MW00946300

Biostatistics MCQs and Explanations for USMLE

These multiple-choice questions COVER THE important CONCEPTS for United States Medical Licensing EXAMINATIONS.

Syed K Haque MD, DABCC, FAACC

website: www.usmlexpert.com
The print version is available on Amazon.com
Last Updated: 2/22/2019

Table of Contents

Epidemiology

Question 1.

Abstract

PURPOSE:

The purpose of this study was to investigate the precise effect of smoking, duration of smoking, and cessation of smoking on the risk of the development of an abdominal aortic aneurysm (AAA).

METHODS:

A nested case control study was carried out in a population-based screening program for men over the age of 50 years. Smoking data were collected by questionnaire, and serum levels of cotinine were used as an objective measure of nicotine exposure.

RESULTS:

Data of 210 cases and 237 control individuals were analyzed. Current smokers were 7.6 times more likely to have an AAA than nonsmokers (95% confidence interval, 3.3%-17.8%). Exsmokers were 3.0 times more likely to have an AAA than nonsmokers (95% confidence interval, 1.4%-6.4%). Duration of smoking was significantly associated with an increased risk of AAA, and there was a clear linear dose response relationship with the duration of smoking; each year of smoking increased the relative risk of AAA by 4% (95% confidence interval, 2%-5%). In contrast, the effect of the amount smoked disappeared when an adjustment was made for the duration of smoking. After the cessation of smoking, there was a very slow decline in the risk of the occurrence of an AAA. Smoking was associated with a higher relative risk of a small aneurysm than a large aneurysm. Serum cotinine levels were higher in men with a small aneurysm than in men with a large aneurysm. Cotinine levels were similar in expanding aneurysms and stable aneurysms.

Abstract Citation: Wilmink TB, Quick CR, Day NE.The association between cigarette smoking and abdominal aortic aneurysms. J Vasc Surg. 1999 Dec;30(6):1099-105.

Which one of the following is the best conclusion that can be drawn from the research abstract above?

- A. Smoking does not cause Abdominal aortic Aneurysm
- B. Smoking has some causal relationship with Abdominal aortic aneurysm
- C. Smoking is not associated with Abdominal aortic aneurysm.
- D. Risk of Abdominal aortic aneurysm was not significantly higher in exsmokers compared to nonsmokers

Explanation

An association between risk factor and outcome as measured by relative risk or odds ratio does not indicate causal relationship. However, presence of dose-response relationship between exposure and outcome is a powerful evidence of causal relationship. The increase in dose could be in the form of levels or duration of exposure. In the above study, there is an increase in the risk of Abdominal Aortic Aneurysm with increased duration of smoking but not with the amount of smoking. This is an evidence of causal relationship (Choice B is the correct answer).

"Ex-smokers were 3.0 times more likely to have a AAA than nonsmokers (95% confidence interval, 1.4%-6.4%)."

Confidence interval is a range of values that is likely to contain the unknown population parameters. Studies are based on a sample of the relevant population. If we are able to design a study to include all ex-smokers in the world, all nonsmokers and all patients with AAA, we will get true relative risk (x)(the population parameter).

"The population parameter is an unknown constant and no probability statement concerning its value may be made." —Jerzy Neyman, original developer of confidence intervals.

So, in the study, 95% confidence interval does not mean that there is 95% probability that the x will fall between 1.4%-6.4%. This is a common misinterpretation of 95% confidence interval.

What does 95% Confidence interval mean?

If we do multiple similar studies, say 20, then 19 out of 20 studies (95% of the studies) will have a confidence interval that has the unknown population parameter. Additionally, 19 out of 20 studies will have a mean (95% of the means) that will fall between 1.4% and 6.4%. In other words, 5% of the means will be outside this range (same as P value= 0.05).

P value and Confidence Interval are used to determine statistical significance. P value is Type 1 error (denoted by the symbol α, discussed elsewhere in the book). 95% Confidence Interval is equivalent to 100%- 5% or 1-0.05 or 1- α .

In studies that calculate relative risk, odds ratio or hazard ratio, if the 95% Confidence interval (the range) is greater than 1 or less than 1 then there is statistical significance. In this study, the range is greater than 1, therefore the relative risk is statistically significant.

Question 2.

Researchers designed a case control study to evaluate several risk factors for stroke. One of the risk factors that was studied is hypertension. With respect to hypertension, they got the following data as shown in the 2 x 2 contingency table.

Hypertension	Stroke		
	Present	absent	Total
present	200	20	220
absent	150	200	350
	350	220	

What is the risk of stroke in a patient with hypertension?

    A. 13.33
    B. 0.48
    C. 20
    D. 2.12

Question 3.

What percentage of the risk of stroke in those with hypertension is attributable to hypertension?

    A. 60
    B. 92
    C. 43.27
    D. 80

Question 4.

What percentage of the risk of stroke in the study population is attributable to hypertension?

    A. 50
    B. 60
    C. 43.27
    D. 92

Question 5.

If we add up the population attributable risk percent of all the known risk factors of stroke, then what value would we get?

    A. Less than 100 %
    B. 100%
    C. More than 100 %
    D. 0%

Explanation

Relative Risk and Odds Ratio are used to quantify risk.

Relative Risk (also termed as Risk Ratio, RR) is the risk of developing harmful event (e.g. disease) in the exposed (or intervention group) compared to the risk in the un-exposed (or control group). This is used in Cohort Study where researchers follow exposed and unexposed cohort of participants (with similar characteristics) and identify those who develop the harmful event.

Odds Ratio (OR) is the odds of the harmful effect (e.g. disease) in those who were exposed to the risk factor under study compared to the odds of the harmful effect in those who were not exposed to that risk factor. This is commonly used in Case Control Study where researchers study the cases (diseased)and healthy controls and look for potential risk factor(s) in them.
In case of very rare outcome (rare diseases), relative risk and odds ratio are almost equal in value and case control study design is more practical.

Let us say researchers exposed X number of participants to the risk factor and Y number of participants were not exposed to the risk factor. These two groups were followed for 10 years and the following results are tabulated in 2x 2 table format.

Researchers use 2x 2 table to present data and determine RR or OR.

Risk Factor	Event		
	Present	absent	Total
present	a	b	X=a+ b
absent	c	d	Y=c+ d
	N1=a+c	N2=b+d	

Relative Risk= (Risk in exposed)/ (Risk in unexposed)
Risk in exposed =   a/ X
Risk in unexposed= c/Y
RR= [a/ X] ÷ [c/Y]

Let us say researchers select N1 number of participants with events and N2 number of participants without the event. These two groups are studied through patient charts and questionnaire to identify those with presence or absence of the risk factor under study. The results are tabulated in 2 x 2 table format.

Risk Factor	Event		
	present	absent	Total
present	a	b	X=a+ b
absent	c	d	Y=c+ d
	N1=a+c	N2=b+d	

OR = Odds of risk factor among those with events ÷ Odds of risk factor among those without events
Odds of risk factor among those with events = a/c
Odds of risk factor among those without events= b/d
OR= a/c ÷ b/d = (a x d) ÷ (b x c)

Alternatively,

OR = Odds of events among those with risk factor ÷ Odds of event among those without risk factor

Odds of events among those with risk factor = a/b

Odds of event among those without risk factor = c/d

OR= a/b ÷ c/d = (a x d) ÷ (b x c)

Attributable Risk is the absolute difference in the incidence of event in exposed group and unexposed group. The risk in the unexposed group is subtracted from the risk in the exposed group. In other word, it is the proportion of risk that is attributable to exposure in the exposed group.

Attributable Risk percent is the attributable risk expressed as a percentage of the risk (or incidence) in the exposed group.

Population Attributable Risk is the absolute difference in the incidence of event in the entire study population (exposed and unexposed group) and unexposed group. The risk in the unexposed group is subtracted from the risk in the study population. In other word, it is the proportion of risk that is attributable to exposure in the study population (exposed and unexposed group).

Population Attributable Fraction (PAF) is the population attributable risk expressed as a proportion of the total risk (or incidence) in the study population (exposed and unexposed group). This epidemiological parameter is used to quantify the contribution of a risk factor to an event. An event can have multiple risk factor. Each risk factor contributes to the event and often interacts with each other. Therefore, adding up the PAF for each risk factors often results in a value greater than 1.

Population Attributable Risk Percent is the population attributable risk expressed as a percentage of the risk (or incidence) in the study population (exposed and unexposed group). An event can have multiple risk factor. Each risk factor contributes to the event and often interacts with each other. Therefore, adding up the PAR % for each risk factors often results in a value greater than 100 % (Question 5, Choice C is correct).

Let us say, researchers investigated the risk of smoking on abdominal aortic aneurysm. A cohort study was carried out. The following data was obtained and tabulated.

Smoking	Abdominal Aortic Aneurysm		
	present	absent	Total
present	a	b	X=a+ b
absent	c	d	Y=c+ d
Population	N1=a+c	N2=b+d	N=N1+N2

Relative Risk= a/X ÷ c/Y (risk in smoker ÷ risk in nonsmoker)

Attributable Risk = a/X- c/Y (risk in smoker- risk in nonsmoker)

Attributable Risk percent = [(a/X-c/Y) ÷ a/X] x 100 = (RR-1)/RR x 100

Population Attributable Risk= N1/N – c/Y

Population attributable risk percent (PAR%) = [(N1/N -c/Y) ÷ N1/N] * 100

In the Question, 2 x 2 table is given. The study design is a case control study. In a case control study, we quantify risk using odds ratio:

Hypertension	Stroke		
	Present	absent	Total
present	200	20	X=220
absent	150	200	Y=350
	350	220	570

Odds ratio = Odds of stroke in those with hypertension ÷ Odds of stroke in those without hypertension= 200/20 ÷ 150/200 = (200 x 200) ÷ (150 x 20) = 13.33 (Question 2, Choice A is correct)

Attributable Risk percent = [(a/b-c/d) ÷ a/b] x 100 = (OR- 1)/OR x 100 = (13.33 -1)/ 13.33 x 100 = 0.92 x 100 = 92% (Question 3, Choice B is correct)

Population attributable risk percent (PAR%)
= [[Odds of stroke in the study population(n=570)- Odds of stroke in those without hypertension]
÷ Odds of stroke in the study population(n=570)] x 100

= [(350/220 – 150/350) ÷ (150/ 350)] x 100 = 0.4327 x 100 = 43.27 % (Question 4, Choice C is correct)

Question 6.

Research Abstract

Background

Tuberculosis is an ancient disease that continues to threaten individual and public health today, especially in sub-Saharan Africa. Current surveillance systems describe general risk of tuberculosis in a population but do not characterize the risk to an individual following exposure to an infectious case.

Methods

In a study of household contacts of infectious tuberculosis cases (n = 1918) and a community survey of tuberculosis infection (N = 1179) in Kampala, Uganda, we estimated the secondary attack rate for tuberculosis disease and tuberculosis infection. The ratio of these rates is the likelihood of progressive primary disease after recent household infection.

Results

The secondary attack rate for tuberculosis disease was 3.0% (95% confidence interval: 2.2, 3.8). The overall secondary attack rate for tuberculosis infection was 47.4 (95% confidence interval: 44.3, 50.6) and did not vary widely with age, HIV status or BCG vaccination. The risk for progressive primary disease was highest among the young or HIV infected and was reduced by BCG vaccination.

Conclusions

Early case detection and treatment may limit household transmission of *M. tuberculosis*. Household members at high risk for disease should be protected through vaccination or treatment of latent tuberculosis infection.

Citation: Whalen CC, Zalwango S, Chiunda A, Malone L, Eisenach K, Joloba M, et al. (2011) Secondary Attack Rate of Tuberculosis in Urban Households in Kampala, Uganda. PLoS ONE 6(2): e16137. doi:10.1371/journal.pone.0016137

Characteristic	Category	No. at Risk	No. Positive Culture Cases	No. without RFLP	No. RFLP Matched Isolates	Estimated No. Matched Isolates†	SAR - Tuberculosis (%)	95% CI
Overall		1918	76	15	46	57.3	3.0	2.2, 3.8
Age (y)	≤5	508	28	3	23	25.8	5.1	3.2, 7.0
	6–15	691	7	3	3	5.3	0.8	0.1, 1.4
	16–25	364	16	3	8	9.8	2.7	1.0, 4.4
	26–45	283	22	5	11	14.2	5.0	2.5, 7.6
	≥46	72	3	1	1	1.5	2.1	0, 5.4
	>5	1410	48	12	23	30.7	2.2	1.4, 2.9
HIV Status	HIV+	201	30	8	13	17.7	8.8	4.9, 12.7
	HIV−	1455	44	7	31	36.9	2.5	1.7, 3.3
BCG Vaccine	Yes	1349	46	6	32	36.8	2.7	1.9, 3.6
	No	499	27	7	13	17.6	3.5	1.9, 5.1

**Co-prevalent cases with the same finger print pattern as the index case. Since 15 cases did not have RLFP results, this number is estimated using the observed proportion (see methods) of RLFP matches. 46/61 observed matches; thus, 46/61*76 culture confirmed cases = 57.3 = 57.

†The total number of cases with matched RFLP patterns is the number of isolates with observed matches plus expected number of matches from isolates grown in culture but not analyzed with RFLP. Expected number of matches was estimated as the product of the observed proportion of matches and the number of pairs without RFLP results plus observed matches.

*HIV serostatus was not available in 262 (13.7%) of contacts. HIV serostatus was not measured in community control households; the general secondary attack rate for infection was therefore used to estimate risk of disease after household infection.

‡Vaccination status missing or uncertain in 70 household contacts and 4 community members.

doi:10.1371/journal.pone.0016137.t001

Based on the research abstract above, what is the relative risk of tuberculosis among the contacts with HIV +ve status?

A. 8.8

B. 2.5

C. 3.5

D. 3.0

Explanation:

		Tuberculosis (based on expected matched isolates)		Secondary Attack Rate
		+	-	
Exposure Status	HIV +	a	b	a/ (a+b) x 100
	HIV -	c	d	c/(c+d) x 100

Secondary attack rate = (new spells within the range of incubation period among those exposed ÷ subjects exposed to the primary cases that can spread the disease) x 100

The following values can be extracted from the abstract:

		Tuberculosis (based on expected matched isolates)		Secondary Attack Rate
		+	-	
Exposure Status	HIV +	17.7(a)	b	a/ (a+b=201) x 100 = 8.8 (**Choice A**)
	HIV -	36.9 (b)	d	c/(c+d= 1445) x 100 = 2.5 (**Choice B**)

Relative risk = Risk of disease in exposed ÷ risk of disease in non-exposed

RR = Risk of disease in HIV + cases ÷ risk of disease in HIV- cases

= Secondary attack rate in HIV + ve ÷ Secondary attack rate in HIV- cases

= 8.8/2.5 = 3.52 (The correct answer)

The overall secondary attack rate is 3.0 (choice D). The correct answer is C.

Attack rate, or **case rate**, is a proportion measuring cumulative incidence often used for particular groups, observed for limited periods and under special circumstances, as in an epidemic; it is usually expressed as percent (cases per 100 in the group).

The **secondary attack rate** is the number of cases among familial or institutional contacts occurring within the accepted incubation period following exposure to a primary case, in relation to the total of exposed contacts; the denominator may be restricted to susceptible contacts when determinable.

Take Home Message

Know the concepts of attack rate, secondary attack rate and relative risk.

Question 7.

Research Abstract

Background

To evaluate the risk and sites of metachronous secondary primary malignancies (SPMs) among patients with esophageal cancer.

Methods

Newly diagnosed esophageal cancer patients between 1997 and 2011 were recruited. To avoid surveillance bias, SPMs that developed within one year were excluded. Standardized incidence ratios (SIRs) of metachronous SPMs in these patients were calculated by comparing to the cancer incidence in the general population. Risk factors for SPM development, included age, sex, comorbidities and cancer-related treatments, were estimated by Cox proportional hazards models.

Results

During the 15-year study period, 870 SPMs developed among 18,026 esophageal cancer patients, with a follow-up of 27,056 person-years. The SIR for all cancers was 3.53. The SIR of follow-up period ≥ 10 years was 3.56; 5–10 years, 3.14; and 1–5 years, 3.06. The cancer SIRs of head and neck (15.83), stomach (3.30), lung and mediastinum (2.10), kidney (2.24) and leukemia (2.72), were significantly increased. Multivariate analysis showed that age ≥ 60 years (hazard ratio [HR] 0.74), being male (HR 1.46) and liver cirrhosis (HR 1.46) were independent factors. According to the treatments, major surgery (HR 1.24) increased the risk, but chemotherapy was nearly significant.

Conclusions

Patients with esophageal cancer were at increased risk of developing metachronous SPMs. The SIR remained high in follow-up > 10 years, so that close monitoring may be needed for early detection of SPM among these esophageal cancer patients.

Citation: Chen S-C, Teng C-J, Hu Y-W, Yeh C-M, Hung M-H, Hu L-Y, et al. (2015) Secondary Primary Malignancy Risk among Patients with Esophageal Cancer in Taiwan: A Nationwide Population-Based Study. PLoS ONE 10(1): e0116384. doi:10.1371/journal.pone.0116384

Based on the research abstract above, what is the expected number of cases of secondary primary malignancies among patients with esophageal cancer?
A. 870
B. 870 x 3.53
C. 870/3.53
D. 870/18026 x 3.53

Explanation:
This question deals with the concept of standardized incidence ratio (SIR).
Standardized Incidence Ratio (SIR) is used to determine if the occurrence of cancer in a relatively small population is high or low. An SIR analysis can tell us if the number of observed cancer cases in a particular geographic area is higher or lower than expected, given the population and age distribution for that community. The expected number is the number of cases that would occur in a smaller community if the age/sex-adjusted incidence rate in a larger reference population (such as the state or country) occurred in that smaller community.

SIR = Observed number of cases/ Expected number of Cases

SIR given in the abstract is 3.53 and observed number of cases is 870.

Therefore,

Expected number of Cases = 870/3.53 (**Choice C**). The correct answer is C.

Take Home Message
SIR = Observed number of cases/ Expected number of Cases

Survival Analysis Interpretation

Question 8.

In a study, researchers were studying the effect of orthostatic hypotension in survival of patients with a neurodegenerative disease. Patients were grouped into those with persistent orthostatic hypotension (n= 100) and with no/mild orthostatic hypotension (100). They were followed for 5 years. At the end of the 5th year, researcher noted that 20 patient from each group had died. What should the researcher do next?

A. Conclude that since the mortality between the group over 5 years follow-up is the same there is no significant effect of orthostatic hypotension on mortality between the two group
B. Perform a time to event analysis
C. Follow up for longer period to rule out latent period
D. Follow up for shorter period

Explanation:

In this study, mortality at the end of 5-year follow-up period is 20% in both group of patients (persistent orthostatic hypotension and no/mild orthostatic hypotension). This seems to suggest that there is no increase in harmful effect in patients with persistent orthostatic hypotension. However, a time to event analysis aka Survival analysis of the two group can reveal significant differences (Choice B).

Survival curve is drawn by plotting survival time on x-axis and survival probability (or proportion of study group(n) surviving) on y-axis as shown in the graph below.

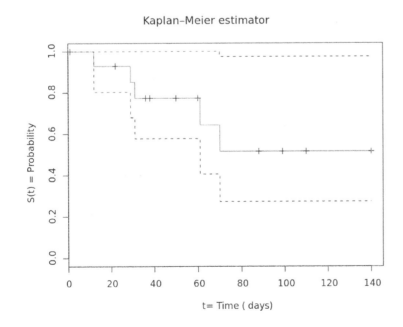

The time it takes for an event such as death to take place is called survival time. Until the first event takes place, the proportion of patient surviving is 1. As time passes, more and more patient die and therefore the proportion surviving decreases until we reach the end of study duration. We cannot determine survival probabilities beyond the study period. Some patients are lost to follow up. These are called censored observation and are shown on the survival curve by tick.

Two Survival curve can be compared to determine significant differences. The most common method used to compare the survival times is the logrank test.

Another important thing to note is that not all survival curve has death as the endpoint (or event). The endpoint, for example, can be response rate or relapse rate.

Survival plot can reveal latent period between two intervention. For example, in the curve below there is no significant difference in survival probability between statin user and non-user in the first several months. This is called latent period. If the study was carried out for a shorter duration, then investigators would have missed the significant difference in survival in the latter months.

Kaplan Meier curves for overall survival in pancreatic cancer patients with statin use and without statin use.

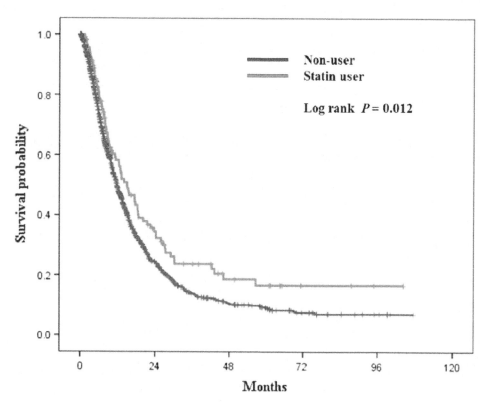

Image Credit:Available via license: CC BY 4.0

Survival plot can plateau at higher survival probability suggesting cure.

Survival plot can reach zero early or later. Every patient dies in this scenario and there is no cure. However, there is longer survival in one group than the other.

Types of Study

Question 9.

In a research study, investigators recruited 400 patients for a randomized controlled trial designed to compare the effectiveness of drug X in reducing LDL level compared to placebo. An intention-to-treat analysis is planned. What type of bias is reduced by this type of analysis?

A. Selection Bias
B. Recall Bias
C. Measurement Bias
D. Confounding Bias
E. Attrition Bias

Explanation

Intention-to Treat analysis concept: "According to Fisher et al. (1990), the ITT analysis includes all randomized patients in the groups to which they were randomly assigned, regardless of their adherence with the entry criteria, regardless of the treatment they actually received, and regardless of subsequent withdrawal **(attrition bias)** from treatment or deviation from the protocol."

Question 10.

Read through this research abstract and answer the question that follow:
Cilostazol for prevention of secondary stroke (CSPS 2): an aspirin-controlled, double-blind, randomised non-inferiority trial. Lancet Neurol. 2010 Oct;9(10):959-68.

Summary
Background
The antiplatelet drug cilostazol is efficacious for prevention of stroke recurrence compared with placebo. We designed the second Cilostazol Stroke Prevention Study (CSPS 2) to establish non-inferiority of cilostazol versus aspirin for prevention of stroke, and to compare the efficacy and safety of cilostazol and aspirin in patients with non-cardioembolic ischaemic stroke.

Methods

Patients aged 20–79 years who had had a cerebral infarction within the previous 26 weeks were enrolled at 278 sites in Japan and allocated to receive 100 mg cilostazol twice daily or 81 mg aspirin once daily for 1–5 years. Patients were allocated according to a computer-generated randomisation sequence by means of a dynamic balancing method using patient information obtained at registration. All patients, study personnel, investigators, and the sponsor were masked to treatment allocation. The primary endpoint was the first occurrence of stroke (cerebral infarction, cerebral haemorrhage, or subarachnoid haemorrhage). The predefined margin of non-inferiority was an upper 95% CI limit for the hazard ratio of 1·33. Analyses were by full-analysis set. This trial is registered with ClinicalTrials.gov, number NCT00234065.

Findings

Between December, 2003, and October, 2006, 2757 patients were enrolled and randomly allocated to receive cilostazol (n=1379) or aspirin (n=1378), of whom 1337 on cilostazol and 1335 on aspirin were included in analyses; mean follow-up was 29 months (SD 16). The primary endpoint occurred at yearly rates of 2·76% (n=82) in the cilostazol group and 3·71% (n=119) in the aspirin group (hazard ratio 0·743, 95% CI 0·564–0·981). Haemorrhagic events (cerebral haemorrhage, subarachnoid haemorrhage, or haemorrhage requiring hospital admission) occurred in fewer patients on cilostazol (0·77%, n=23) than on aspirin (1·78%, n=57; 0·458, 0·296–0·711; p=0·0004), but headache, diarrhoea, palpitation, dizziness, and tachycardia were more frequent in the cilostazol group than in the aspirin group.

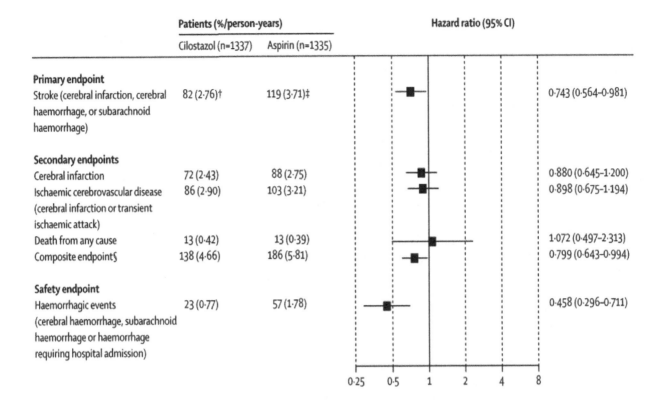

Patients (%/person-years)		Hazard ratio (95% CI)
Cilostazol (n=1337)	Aspirin (n=1335)	

Primary endpoint

Stroke (cerebral infarction, cerebral haemorrhage, or subarachnoid haemorrhage): Cilostazol 82 (2·76)†, Aspirin 119 (3·71)‡ — 0·743 (0·564–0·981)

Secondary endpoints

Cerebral infarction: Cilostazol 72 (2·43), Aspirin 88 (2·75) — 0·880 (0·645–1·200)

Ischaemic cerebrovascular disease (cerebral infarction or transient ischaemic attack): Cilostazol 86 (2·90), Aspirin 103 (3·21) — 0·898 (0·675–1·194)

Death from any cause: Cilostazol 13 (0·42), Aspirin 13 (0·39) — 1·072 (0·497–2·313)

Composite endpoint§: Cilostazol 138 (4·66), Aspirin 186 (5·81) — 0·799 (0·643–0·994)

Safety endpoint

Haemorrhagic events (cerebral haemorrhage, subarachnoid haemorrhage or haemorrhage requiring hospital admission): Cilostazol 23 (0·77), Aspirin 57 (1·78) — 0·458 (0·296–0·711)

Which of the following best describes the effect of Cilostazol in the prevention of Stroke?

A. Cilostazol is non-inferior and not superior to Aspirin
B. The result is inconclusive
C. Cilostazol is non-inferior and inferior to Aspirin
D. Cilostazol is non-inferior and superior to Aspirin
E. Cilostazol is inferior and not non inferior to Aspirin

Explanation:
This question tests your ability to interpret studies that use non-inferiority clinical trials. Efficacy of an experimental treatment is most convincingly established by demonstrating its superiority to a placebo in a placebo-controlled trial, by showing superiority to an active control treatment, or by demonstrating a dose-response relationship. This type of trial is referred to as a superiority trial.

However, if the intent of a study is to demonstrate that an experimental treatment is not substantially worse than a control treatment, the study is known as a non-inferiority trial. In other words, **non-inferiority trials test whether a new experimental treatment (Cilostazol, in the above abstract) is not unacceptably less efficacious than an active control treatment (Aspirin,in the above abstract) already in use.** Sometimes assigning patients to a placebo is unethical. In such circumstances, there has been increasing emphasis on the use of non-inferiority trial designs. The term "active control trial" refers to clinical trials in which the control treatment employed is an active one.

If the intent of a study is to demonstrate that differences between control and experimental treatments are not large in either direction, then it is known as an equivalence trial. Bioequivalence trials are those in which generic drug preparations are compared to currently marketed formulations.

Interpretation of Non-Inferiority Trials

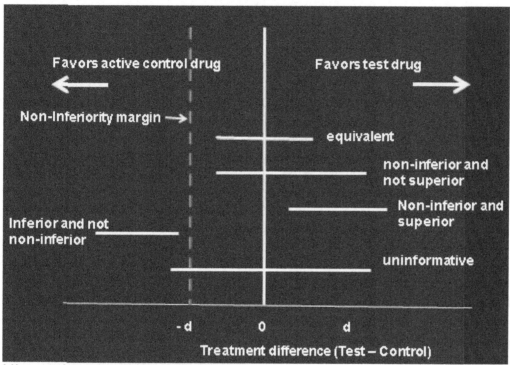

NI margin= Non-Inferiority Margin

In this question, the non-inferiority margin is stated as *"The predefined margin of non-inferiority was an upper 95% CI limit for the hazard ratio of 1·33"*. The figure shows the hazard ratio (including the confidence interval) of Cilostazol compared to Aspirin for stroke to be less than 1 and less than 1.33(the non-inferiority margin); therefore, Cilostazol is superior and non-inferior to Aspirin for Stroke. If it was more than 1.33, then it would have been "inferior and non-inferior".

A hazard ratio of less than 1 is preventive and favors test drug (Cilostazol in the above case) whereas a hazard ratio of greater than 1 is detrimental and would favor control drug (Aspirin in the above case).

Question 11.

Take a look at the following figure from the above study.

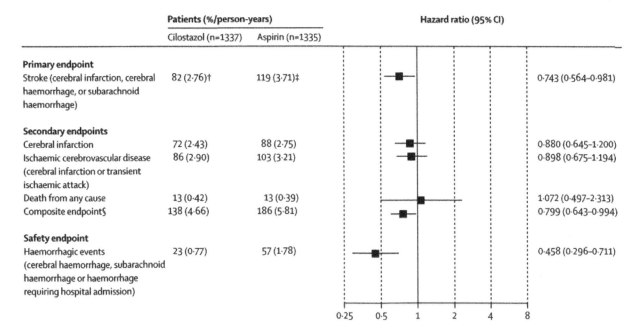

	Patients (%/person-years)		Hazard ratio (95% CI)
	Cilostazol (n=1337)	Aspirin (n=1335)	
Primary endpoint			
Stroke (cerebral infarction, cerebral haemorrhage, or subarachnoid haemorrhage)	82 (2·76)†	119 (3·71)‡	0·743 (0·564–0·981)
Secondary endpoints			
Cerebral infarction	72 (2·43)	88 (2·75)	0·880 (0·645–1·200)
Ischaemic cerebrovascular disease (cerebral infarction or transient ischaemic attack)	86 (2·90)	103 (3·21)	0·898 (0·675–1·194)
Death from any cause	13 (0·42)	13 (0·39)	1·072 (0·497–2·313)
Composite endpoint§	138 (4·66)	186 (5·81)	0·799 (0·643–0·994)
Safety endpoint			
Haemorrhagic events (cerebral haemorrhage, subarachnoid haemorrhage or haemorrhage requiring hospital admission)	23 (0·77)	57 (1·78)	0·458 (0·296–0·711)

Which of the following best describes the effect of Cilostazol in the prevention of Cerebral Infarction?

A. Aspirin is better than Cilostazol

B. Cilostazol is better than Aspirin

C. Cilostazol is non-inferior and inferior

D. Cilostazol is superior and non-inferior

E. Cilostazol is non-inferior and not superior

Explanation

Interpretation of Non-Inferiority Trials

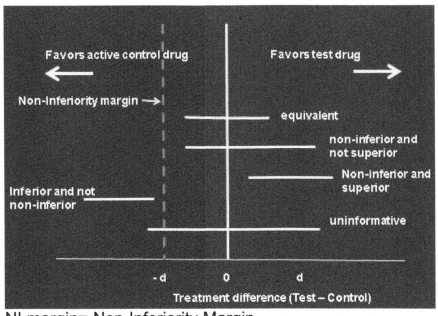

NI margin= Non-Inferiority Margin

In this question, the non-inferiority margin is stated as *"The predefined margin of non-inferiority was an upper 95% CI limit for the hazard ratio of 1·33"*. The figure shows the hazard ratio (including the confidence interval) of Cilostazol compared to Aspirin for cerebral infarction to be more than 1 and less than 1.33(the non-inferiority margin) (mean 0.880, CI 0.645-1.200); therefore, Cilostazol is "not superior and non-inferior" to Aspirin for cerebral infarction. If it was more than 1.33, then it would have been "inferior and non-inferior" (**Choice C**).

A hazard ratio of less than 1 is preventive and favors test drug (Cilostazol in the above case) whereas a hazard ratio of greater than 1 is detrimental and would favor control drug (Aspirin in the above case).

Question 12.

A group of researchers were examining the risk of Alzheimer's disease with Vaccine X. 300 subjects were given vaccine and 300 were given placebo. They were followed for 10 years. They got the following data:

	Alzheimer	No Alzheimer
Vaccine	100	200
Placebo	50	250

A review of literature revealed that hormone replacement therapy is also associated with Alzheimer disease. The researchers rearranged the data according to hormone replacement therapy as follows:

Subjects taking Hormone Replacement Therapy:

	Alzheimer	No Alzheimer
Vaccine	50	150
Placebo	50	150

Subjects who were not taking Hormone Replacement Therapy:

	Alzheimer	No Alzheimer
Vaccine	25	75
Placebo	25	75

What type of study did the researcher conduct?
A. Cross-sectional Study
B. Case-control Study
C. Cohort Study
D. Twin concordance study
E. Adoption study
F. Cross Over Study

Explanation:
A cohort study is a study design where one or more cohorts (group(s) with similar characteristics) are followed prospectively or retrospectively and are evaluated with respect to a disease or outcome to determine which initial participants exposure characteristics (risk factors) are associated with the disease (or predefined outcome).Unlike in case-control study, in this type of study the outcome is not known at the start of the study. The correct answer is C.

Cross-sectional study (**Choice A**) is a type of observational study that involves the analysis of data collected from a population at one specific point in time. Example: disease prevalence

Case-control study (**Choice B**) is designed to help determine if an exposure is associated with an outcome. In this type of study, the outcome (such as disease) is known to the investigator. So, it is always retrospective. Investigators look back at previously collected data (such as medical record) to determine exposure to risk factors in those with the disease and those without.

Twin concordance study (**Choice D**) compares the frequency with which twins (monozygotic or dizygotic) develop the same disease.

Adoption Study (**Choice E**) compares siblings raised by biological parents with those by adoptive parents.

Cross Over Study (**Choice F**) is a longitudinal study in which subjects receive a sequence of different treatments or exposures. An example would be when two groups of participants, A and B, receive drug X and placebo for the first 6 months and then after a wash out period of a week, the treatment regimen is switched between the two group for the next 6 month (see figure below).

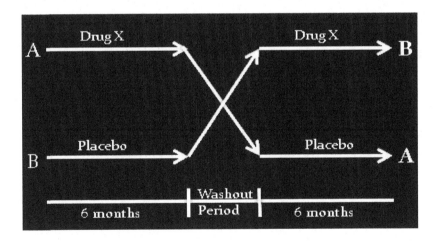

Take Home Message
A cohort study is a study design where one or more cohorts (group(s) with similar characteristics) are followed prospectively or retrospectively and are evaluated with respect to a disease or outcome to determine which initial participants exposure characteristics (risk factors) are associated with the disease (or predefined outcome).Unlike in case-control study, in this type of study the outcome is not known at the start of the study.

Question 13.

J Lipid Res. 2018 May;59(5):872-883. doi: 10.1194/jlr.P080143. Epub 2018 Mar 25.

Apolipoprotein-defined lipoprotein subclasses, serum apolipoproteins, and carotid intima-media thickness in T1D.

Basu A, Jenkins AJ, Stoner JA, Zhang Y, Klein RL, Lopes-Virella MF, Garvey WT, Schade DS, Wood J, Alaupovic P, Lyons TJ; Diabetes Control and Complications Trial/Epidemiology of Diabetes Interventions and Complications Research Group.

Abstract

Circulating apolipoprotein-defined lipoprotein subclasses (ADLS) and apolipoproteins predict vascular events in the general and type 2 diabetes populations, but data in T1D are limited. We examined associations of ADLS, serum apolipoproteins, and conventional lipids with carotid intima-media thickness (IMT) measured contemporaneously and 6 years later in 417 T1D participants [men: n = 269, age 42 ± 6 y (mean ± SD); women: n = 148, age 39 ± 8 y] in the Epidemiology of Diabetes Interventions and Complications study, the follow-up of the Diabetes Control and Complications Trial (DCCT). Date were analyzed by multiple linear regression stratified by sex, and adjusted for time-averaged hemoglobin A1C, diabetes duration, hypertension, BMI, albuminuria, DCCT randomization, smoking, statin treatment, and ultrasound devices. In cross-sectional analyses, lipoprotein B (Lp-B), Lp-B:C, Lp-B:E+Lp-B:C:E, Apo-A-II, Apo-B, Apo-C-III-HP (heparin precipitate; i.e., Apo-C-III in Apo-B-containing lipoproteins), and Apo-E were positively associated with common and/or internal carotid IMT in men, but only Apo-C-III (total) was (positively) associated with internal carotid IMT in women. In prospective analyses, Lp-B, Apo-B, and Apo-C-III-HP were positively associated with common and/or internal carotid IMT in men, while Lp-A1:AII and Apo-A1 were inversely associated with internal carotid IMT in women. The only significant prospective association between conventional lipids and IMT was between triacylglycerols and internal carotid IMT in men. ADLS and apolipoprotein concentrations may provide sex-specific biomarkers and suggest mechanisms for IMT in people with T1D.

Which of the following best describes the study design ?

A. Crossover
B. Cross-Sectional
C. Factorial

D. Nested
E. Pragmatic

Explanation:

A nested case control (NCC) study is a variation of a case-control study in which cases and controls are drawn from the population in a bigger cohort. Usually, the exposure of interest is only measured among the cases and controls of only 2-3 times that of cases are selected from the bigger cohort which could go into thousands. This is more cost effective. The correct answer is Nested.

When you have multiple independent variables in a single study, it is called **factorial design**. Example: Effect of more than one independent variable such as exercise, food and gender on a dependent variable such LDL.

Pragmatic Clinical Trial (PCT) is an alternative to Randomized Clinical Trial(RCT). PCTs take place in the setting where patients already receive their usual clinical care. Interventions, follow-up, and adherence protocols are aligned with usual care. This gives a better understanding of the implications of the intervention in actual clinical care scenario.

Bias and Study Errors

Question 14.

A group of researchers were examining the risk of Alzheimer's disease with Vaccine X. 300 subjects were given vaccine and 300 were given placebo. They were followed for 10 years. They got the following data:

	Alzheimer	No Alzheimer
Vaccine	100	200
Placebo	50	250

A review of literature revealed that hormone replacement therapy is also associated with Alzheimer disease. The researchers rearranged the data according to hormone replacement therapy as follows:
Subjects taking Hormone Replacement Therapy:

	Alzheimer	No Alzheimer
Vaccine	50	150
Placebo	50	150

Subjects who were not taking Hormone Replacement Therapy:

	Alzheimer	No Alzheimer

Vaccine	25	75
Placebo	25	75

The stratified result is explained by which of the following?
A.   Selection bias
B.   Recall bias
C.   Measurement bias
D.   Pygmalion effect
E.   Confounding bias
F.   Effect modification
G.   Hawthorne effect

Explanation:

In a cohort study, risk is quantified using Relative Risk.

	Alzheimer	No Alzheimer
Vaccine	100	200
Placebo	50	250

In the non-stratified data,

Risk of Alzheimer in those who got vaccine = 100/ (100 + 200) = 1/3
Risk of Alzheimer in those who got placebo = 50/ (50 + 250) = 1/6
Therefore, Relative risk (RR) of Alzheimer with vaccine
= (Risk of Alzheimer in those who got vaccine) / (Risk of Alzheimer in those who got placebo)
= (1/3) ÷ (1/6) = 6/3 = 2

Those who took vaccine were 2 times more likely to develop Alzheimer than those who took placebo.

Relative Risk for stratified data:

Subjects taking Hormone Replacement Therapy (HRT):
RR = (Risk of Alzheimer in those on HRT who got vaccine) / (Risk of Alzheimer in those on HRT who got placebo)
= (50/ (50+150)) ÷ (50/ (50+150)) = 1

Subjects not taking Hormone Replacement Therapy (HRT):
RR = (Risk of Alzheimer in those not on HRT who got vaccine) / (Risk of Alzheimer in those not on HRT who got placebo)
= (25/(25+75)) ÷ (25/(25+75)) = 1

Thus, stratified analysis shows that relative risk of Alzheimer in HRT group and non-HRT group is neutral that is 1. Therefore, the finding of RR of 2 in those who got vaccine in crude analysis was incorrect because of the confounding factor of Hormone Replacement Therapy. The correct answer is E.

Selection Bias (**Choice A**) occurs from nonrandom assignment of participants in study groups.

Recall Bias (**Choice B**) occurs when awareness of the disease and risk factors alters recall by the subject.

Measurement Bias (**Choice C**) occurs when groups who know they are being studied behave differently and thus it results in distortion of the data.

Pygmalion Effect (**Choice D**) occurs when investigators believe that certain treatment is effective and thus is more likely to report positive outcome.

Effect modification **(Choice F)**: If the relative risk had increased or decreased significantly in Hormone Replacement Therapy group then it would have been classified as effect modification.

Hawthorne effect **(Choice G)** is the tendency of study group to change their behavior when they know they are being studied.

Take Home Message
Know how to calculate relative risk and different types of bias and study errors.

Question 15.

A group of researchers were examining the risk of Alzheimer's disease with Vaccine X. 300 subjects were given vaccine and 300 were given placebo. They were followed for 10 years. They got the following data:

	Alzheimer	No Alzheimer
Vaccine	100	200
Placebo	50	250

A review of literature revealed that smoking is also associated with Alzheimer disease. The researchers rearranged the data according to smoking as follows:

Subjects who were currently smoking:

	Alzheimer	No Alzheimer
Vaccine	75	150
Placebo	25	150

Subjects who were not currently smoking:

	Alzheimer	No Alzheimer
Vaccine	25	75
Placebo	25	75

The stratified result is explained by which of the following?
A. Selection bias
B. Recall bias
C. Measurement bias

D. Pygmalion effect
E. Confounding bias
F. Effect modification
G. Hawthorne effect

Explanation:
In a cohort study, risk is quantified using Relative Risk.

	Alzheimer	No Alzheimer
Vaccine	100	200
Placebo	50	250

In the non-stratified data,
Risk of Alzheimer in those who got vaccine = $100/(100 + 200) = 1/3$
Risk of Alzheimer in those who got placebo = $50/(50 + 250) = 1/6$
Therefore, Relative risk (RR) of Alzheimer with vaccine
= (Risk of Alzheimer in those who got vaccine) / (Risk of Alzheimer in those who got placebo)
= $(1/3) ÷ (1/6) = 6/3 = 2$

Those who took vaccine were 2 times more likely to develop Alzheimer than those who took placebo.
Relative Risk for stratified data:

Subjects who were active smokers:
RR = (Risk of Alzheimer in active smokers who got vaccine) / (Risk of Alzheimer in active smokers who got placebo)
= $(75/(75+150)) ÷ (25/(25+150)) = (75/225) / (25/175) = 0.33/0.14 = 2.35$

Subjects who were not active smokers:
RR = (Risk of Alzheimer in those who were not active smokers who got vaccine) / (Risk of Alzheimer in those who were not active smokers who got placebo)
= $(25/(25+75)) ÷ (25/(25+75)) = 1$

Thus, stratified analysis shows that relative risk of Alzheimer in smokers is higher than crude analysis. This is effect modification. The correct answer is F.

Selection Bias (**Choice A**) occurs from nonrandom assignment of participants in study groups.
Recall Bias (**Choice B**) occurs when awareness of the disease and risk factors alters recall by the subject.
Measurement Bias (**Choice C**) occurs when groups who know they are being studied behave differently and thus it results in distortion of the data.
Pygmalion Effect (**Choice D**) occurs when investigators believe that certain treatment is effective and thus is more likely to report positive outcome.

The stratified analysis did not show relative risk of Alzheimer in active smoker and non-active smoker to be neutral that is 1. The sub-analysis showed an increase in relative risk (2.25). Thus smoking is an effect modifier and not a confounding factor (**Choice E**).

Hawthorne effect (**Choice G**) is the tendency of study group to change their behavior when they know they are being studied.

Take Home Message
Know how to calculate relative risk and different types of bias and study errors.

Question 16

Conventional pharmacotherapies and psychotherapies for major depression are associated with limited adherence to care and relatively low remission rates. Yoga may offer an alternative treatment option, but rigorous studies are few. This randomized controlled trial with blinded outcome assessors examined an 8-week hatha yoga intervention as mono-therapy for mild-to-moderate major depression.

Enrollment

Over a 5-month recruitment period, 97 individuals were screened for eligibility. A total of 59 individuals were excluded from study participation. A total of 38 participants met inclusion criteria and were randomized to study interventions, with 20 participants allocated to the yoga group and 18 participants allocated to the attention control group. Among those randomized, 8 participants never started their allocated interventions (n = 2 in yoga group, n = 6 in control group). An additional 5 participants dropped out before the final session at 8 weeks (n = 3 in yoga group, n = 2 in control group). Thus, a total of 13 participants were lost to follow-up (n = 5 in yoga group, n = 8 in control group). Final 8-week measures were obtained from 75% (n = 15) in the yoga group, 56% (n = 10) in the control group, and 66% (n = 25) in the total sample.

Results are as tabulated as follows:

Time	Adjusted Mean BDI Score [95% CI]		8-wk BDI Change Score [95% CI]	
	Yoga Practice Group, n = 20	Attention Control Group, n = 18	Yoga Practice Group, n = 20	Attention Control Group, n = 18
Baseline	20.98 [18.45, 23.51]	19.92 [17.26, 22.58]	-9.47 [-12.37, -6.57]	- 2.99 [-6.43, -0.45]
2 wks	15.15 [12.17, 18.12]	13.06 [8.91, 17.20]		
4 wks	14.35 [11.28, 17.41]	14.66 [10.76, 18.56]		
6 wks	13.04 [9.46, 16.62]	12.72 [7.82, 17.62]		
8 wks	11.51 [8.69, 14.33]	16.93 [13.56, 20.30]		

https://doi.org/10.1371/journal.pone.0173869.t003

(Prathikanti S, Rivera R, Cochran A, Tungol JG, Fayazmanesh N, Weinmann E (2017) Treating major depression with yoga: A prospective, randomized, controlled pilot trial. PLoS ONE 12(3): e0173869.
https://doi.org/10.1371/journal.pone.0173869)

A BDI score of 0-13 is minimal depression and anything above 13 is significant depression (mild, moderate or severe). Assume the following additional results (not reported in the study), at the end of 8 weeks, 2 participants in the yoga arm have BDI score > 13 and 15 participants in the attention control arm have BDI score >13. Of the 15 who completed the yoga arm study, no one had BDI score > 13. Of the 10 who completed, attention control arm of the study, all 10 had BDI score >13. Between 2-4 weeks, 3 subjects switched to attention control arm (all had BDI > 13 at 8 weeks) and 2 switched to yoga group arm (1 had BDI > 13 at 8 weeks).

If the investigators were to use intention-to-treat analysis, what would be the relative risk reduction?
A. 0.10
B. 0.83
C. 0.12
D. 0.88

Question 17

In the above example, if the investigators were to use "per protocol" analysis, what would be the relative risk reduction?

A. 0.00
B. 1.00
C. 0.80
D. 0.50

Question 18

In the above example, if the investigators were to use "as treated" analysis, what would be the relative risk reduction?

A. 0.06
B. 1.00
C. 0.94
D. 0.88

Question 19

What type of analysis is the best in the above example?

A. Intention to Treat Analysis

B. Per protocol Analysis
C. As Treated Analysis
D. Post Hoc Analysis
E. A Priori

Explanation:

Intention to Treat Analysis stipulates that we count all events in randomized groups regardless of whether they received the interventions. This type of analysis is used in randomized controlled trial when there is non-compliance, protocol deviation, withdrawal, missing outcome or anything else.

Per protocol Analysis includes only those subjects who have completed the study in accordance with the protocol. It excludes all those who have been non-compliant, deviated from the protocol, and withdrew.

As treated Analysis includes all those subjects who have received or not received interventions regardless of the initial randomization such as switching between the treatment and control arms.

Post Hoc Analysis is data analysis to test a new hypothesis that was not determined before the data was seen. In a typical study, we have a hypothesis. We design study and collect data. We then analyze the data to test the hypothesis. In Post Hoc Analysis, while looking at the data we come up with another hypothesis and then we analyze the data again to test that new hypothesis.

A priori power analysis is conducted prior to the research study to estimate sample sizes to achieve predefined power. **Post-hoc power analysis** is conducted after a study has been completed to determine what the power was in the study based on sample size and effect size in the study.

Intention to Treat Analysis gives a conservative estimate of the **Relative Risk Reduction** and is hence the best analysis in the above situation.

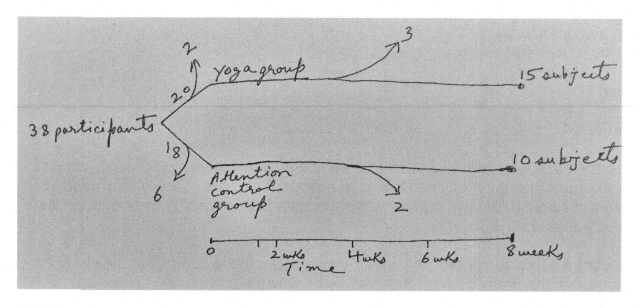

Relative Risk Reduction (RRR) is the proportion of risk reduction that is attributable to the intervention as compared to control.

Relative Risk (RR), used in cohort studies, is the risk of developing disease (or harm) in the exposed group (or intervention group) divided by risk in the unexposed group (or control group).

RRR= 1- RR

Question 16 Answer
Intention to Treat Analysis

Randomization: 20 in yoga group and 18 in Attention control group
Yoga Group Risk = 2/ 20 = 0.1 (2 subjects had >13 BDI)
Attention Control Group Risk = 15/18 = 0.83 (15 subjects had >13 BDI)
RR= 0.1/0.83 = 0.12
RRR= 1- 0.12 = 0.88 (is the answer)

Question 17 Answer
Per protocol Analysis
In protocol: 15 in yoga group and 10 in attention control group
Yoga Group Risk = 0/ 15 = 0.0 (0 subjects had >13 BDI)
Attention Control Group Risk = 10/10 = 1.00 (10 subjects had >13 BDI)
RR= 0.0/1.00 = 0.00
RRR= 1- 0.00 = 1.00 (is the answer)

Question 18 Answer
As Treated Analysis
In Treatment: 17 in yoga group and 13 in attention control group as 2 switched to yoga group and 3 switched to attention control group.

Yoga Group Risk = 1/ 17 = 0.06 (1 subject had >13 BDI)
Attention Control Group Risk = 13/13 = 1.00 (13 subjects had >13 BDI)
RR= 0.06/1.00 = 0.06
RRR= 1- 0.06 = 0.94 (is the answer)

Take Home Message
Intention to Treat (ITT) analysis includes all intervention and control subjects that were randomized at the start of the study regardless of their adherence with the entry criteria, the treatment they actually receive, withdrawal from treatment or any other deviation from the protocol. It works best when the outcome of those who deviated from the protocol is known and provides a conservative estimate of the relative risk reduction.

Question 20

A 34-year-old male arrived in an ambulance in the emergency department. He had headache, dizziness, nausea, vomiting, vertigo, ataxia and nystagmus. He was given aspirin as a suspected case of stroke. He said it all started after he moved his head to the side. He was later diagnosed as Benign Paroxysmal Positional Vertigo and discharged with appropriate medicines for the same. Two days later he was brought to the emergency again with similar symptom. The attending physician was told another doctor two days ago had thought that he had Benign Paroxysmal Positional Vertigo. He diagnosed him with Benign Paroxysmal Positional Vertigo and discharged him home. Two days later he was brought to the emergency department again and died an hour later. Autopsy showed he had cerebellar infarction.
The physician's decision in the second emergency department visit can be described as which one of the followings?

A. Availability Bias
B. Anchoring Effect
C. Framing Effect
D. Overconfidence

Explanation:

Cognitive biases are errors in thinking that influence how we make decisions. Studies have attributed a lot of diagnostic inaccuracies and suboptimal management to the presence of cognitive biases in physicians. Some of the most common cognitive biases are as follows:

Anchoring Effect or focalism is when a person relies too heavily, or "anchor," on one piece of information when making decisions. In the above case, the physician relied on the statement that another doctor had diagnosed the patient with BPPV two days ago. The correct answer is anchoring effect.

Availability Bias: The availability heuristic is a mental shortcut that relies on immediate examples that come to a given person's mind (because of being recalled easily) when evaluating a decision.

Framing effect: The framing effect is when people react to a particular choice in different ways depending on how it is presented; e.g. positively or negatively.

Overconfidence: The overconfidence effect is when a person's subjective confidence in his judgements is greater than the objective accuracy of those judgements.

Other examples of cognitive bias that could cause a physician to make diagnostic or therapeutic errors are: **Omission Bias, Blind Obedience, Commission Bias, Confirmation Bias, Diagnostic Bias/premature closing, Tolerance to risk, Satisfying Bias**

Evaluation of Diagnostic Tests

Question 21.

In a research study, the diagnostic performance of Macrophage inhibitory cytokine 1 (MIC-1), CA19.9, CEA and CA242 was evaluated. The following figure shows the data analysis from the study.

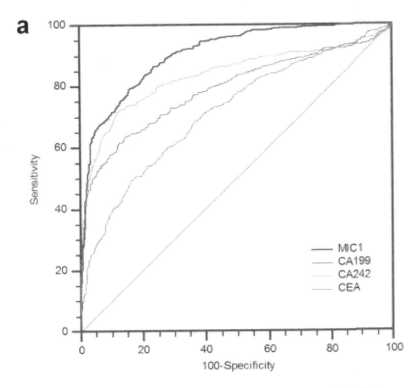

Area under receiver operating characteristic curve (AUROC)					
	AUC	SE	P value	95% CI	
				lower	up
MIC1	0.935	0.0065		0.920	0.948
CA199	0.803	0.0119	< 0.001	0.780	0.824
CA242	0.848	0.0107	< 0.001	0.828	0.867
CEA	0.725	0.0137	< 0.001	0.700	0.749

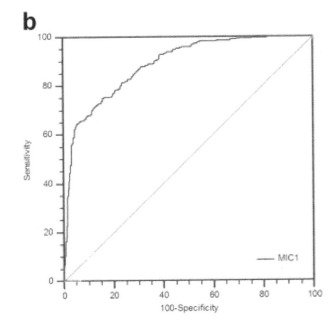

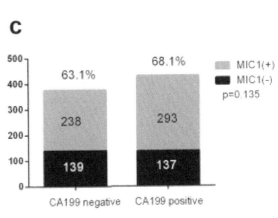

Figure. Comparison of the diagnostic performance of serum MIC-1, CA19.9, CEA and CA242 for PDAC. a. Sensitivities and specificities of MIC-1 , CA19.9, CEA and CA242 for the diagnosis of pancreatic ductal adenocarcinoma (PDAC) was compared through the analyses of ROC curves in the discovery group (n = 1307). AUROC curve of serum MIC-1 was much larger than that of CA19.9, CEA and CA242 (P < 0.001). **b**. The potential of serum MIC-1 for distinguishing CA19.9-negative pancreatic carcinomas from non–pancreatic carcinoma controls including benign pancreas tumors. **c**. A similar positive rate (present above the bar) of serum MIC-1 (using the cut off value 1000 pg/mL) was observed in patients with PDAC with different CA19.9 levels (Ref: Ann R Coll Surg Engl. 2013 April; 95(3): 215–221.)

Based on the study, which one of the following is the most accurate diagnostic test for pancreatic ductal adenocarcinoma?

A. MIC-1
B. CA19.9
C. CEA
D. CA242

Receiver Operating Characteristic curve (ROC curve) is used to compare the performance of different tests. The tests with the greatest area under the curve (AUC) is considered the most accurate.

ROC curve is a plot of true positive rate against the false positive rate for the different possible cut off level of a diagnostic test. True positive rate is the same as sensitivity and false positive rate is 100-specificity (in %age).
The closer the curve comes to the 45-degree diagonal of the ROC space, the less accurate the test. The correct answer is A.

Question 22

Abstract

Background

This study compared TB diagnostic tools and estimated levels of misdiagnosis in a resource-limited setting. Furthermore, we estimated the diagnostic utility of three-TB-associated predictors in an algorithm with and without Direct Ziehl-Neelsen (DZM).
Materials and Methods

Data was obtained from a cross-sectional study in 2011 conducted at Mubende regional referral hospital in Uganda. An individual was included if they presented with a two weeks persistent cough and or lymphadenitis/abscess. 344 samples were analyzed on DZM in Mubende and compared to duplicates analyzed on direct fluorescent microscopy (DFM), growth on solid and liquid media at Makerere University. Clinical variables from a questionnaire and DZM were used to predict TB status in multivariable logistic and Cox proportional hazard models, while optimization and visualization was done with receiver operating characteristics curve and algorithm-charts in Stata, R and Lucid-Charts respectively.

Results are shown in the Table below:

Evaluated test	Gold standard		
	DZM/DFM*	DZM/LJ	DFM/LJ
	Positive Negative	Positive Negative	Positive Negative
Positive	25 7	24 8	53 8
Negative	36 276	42 270	13 270
		Estimate (95%CI)	Estimate (95%CI)
Sensitivity (%)		36.4(24.9–49.1)	80.3(68.7–89.1)
Specificity (%)		97.1(94.4–98.7)	97.1((94.4–98.7)
Positive predictive value (%)		75.1(56.6–88.5)	86.9(75.8–94.2)
Negative predictive value (%)		86.5(82.2–90.1)	95.4(92.3–97.5)
Kappa agreement measure (%)		41.6(36.6–46.6)	79.7(74.3–85.1)

*DFM is used as the gold standard with DZM. Note that the rest of the comparison is done with Results on LJ media as the gold standard. The status (+/−) of the reference tool will be the column status while the test tool is the row. For example (DZM/DFM) = row (+/−)/col(+/−).
doi:10.1371/journal.pone.0100720.t002

Table . Diagnostic performance of DZM&DFM against culture on LJ (gold standard) in detection of bacilli in clinical samples obtained from patients at Mubende referral hospital, Uganda.

Citation: Muwonge A, Malama S, Bronsvoort BMdC, Biffa D, Ssengooba W, Skjerve E (2014) A Comparison of Tools Used for Tuberculosis Diagnosis in Resource-Limited Settings: A Case Study at Mubende Referral Hospital, Uganda. PLoS ONE 9(6): e100720. doi:10.1371/journal.pone.0100720

Based on the above study, what is negative likelihood ratio of direct fluorescent microscopy for TB?

A. 0.80/0.03

B. 0.20/0.97

C. 0.03

D. 0.20

Explanation

This question is asking the probability of negative direct fluorescent microscopy in a tuberculosis patient compared to the probability of negative direct fluorescent microscopy in a healthy control.

Negative likelihood ratio (LR-) is the probability of a person who has the disease testing negative divided by the probability of a person who does not have the disease testing negative.

LR- = (1- sensitivity) / specificity

Sensitivity for DFM = 80.3% or 0.80
Specificity for DFM= 97.1% or 0.97
= (1- 0.80)/(0.97) = **0.20/0.97 (The correct choice).** The correct answer is B.
0.20 is the false negative rate (**Choice D**)
LR+ is the probability of a person who has the disease testing positive divided by the probability of a person who does not have the disease testing positive.

LR+ = sensitivity/ (1- specificity)
Sensitivity for DFM = 80.3% or 0.80
Specificity for DFM= 97.1% or 0.97
= (0.80)/(1-0.97) = **0.80/0.03** (**Choice A**)
0.03 is the false positive rate (**Choice C**).
Another example,
In a 2x2 table, the calculation of likelihood ratio is shown below.

		Cervical Cancer by Gold standard test		Total	
		+ve	-ve		
Diagnostic Test	+ve	10 (True positive)	40 (False positive)	50	PPV= **True positive**/(True positive + False Positive)
	-ve	5 (False negative)	45 (True negative)	50	NPV= **True negative**/(True negative + False negative)
		15	85	100	
		Sensitivity= **True positive**/(True positive + False negative)	Specificity= **True negative**/(True negative + False Positive)		**LR+ = TPR/FPR**
					LR- = FNR/TNR

Take home message:
Negative likelihood ratio (LR-) is the probability of a person who has the disease testing negative divided by the probability of a person who does not have the disease testing negative.

LR- = (1- sensitivity) / specificity

Question 23.

Read the research abstract below and answer the question that follow:

Research Abstract

High mobility group box 1 protein (HMGB1), a nuclear protein, can be translocated to the cytoplasm and secreted in colon cancer cells. However, the diagnostic significance of HMGB1 has not been evaluated in colorectal carcinomas. For this purpose, we have screened the expression and secretion of HMGB1 in 10 colon cancer cell lines and 1 control cell line and found that HMGB1 was detected in the culture medium. To evaluate the diagnostic value of HMGB1, we performed an enzyme-linked immunosorbent assay to measure HMGB1 levels and compared them to carcinoembryonic antigen (CEA) levels in the serum samples of 219 colorectal carcinoma patients and 75 healthy control subjects. We found that the serum HMGB1 level was increased by 1.5-fold in patients with colorectal carcinoma compared to those in healthy controls. When HMGB1 and CEA levels were compared, HMGB1 had similar efficacy as CEA regarding cancer detection (the sensitivity was 20.1% for HMGB1 vs. 25.6% for CEA, and the specificity was 96% for HMGB1 vs. 90.7% for CEA). Moreover, the diagnostic accuracy of HMGB1 for stage I cancer was significantly higher than that of CEA (sensitivity: 41.2% vs. 5.9%; specificity: 96% vs. 90.7). When we combined HMGB1 and CEA, the overall diagnostic sensitivity was higher than that of CEA alone (42% vs. 25.6%), and the diagnostic sensitivity for stage I was also elevated (47% vs. 5.9%). However, the prognosis of patients was not related with serum HMGB1 concentrations. Our findings indicate that serum HMGB1 levels are increased in a subset of colorectal carcinomas, suggesting their potential utility as a supportive diagnostic marker for colorectal carcinomas. (Lee H, Song M, Shin N, Shin CH, Min BS, Kim H-S, et al. (2012) Diagnostic Significance of Serum HMGB1 in Colorectal Carcinomas. PLoS ONE 7(4): e34318. doi:10.1371/journal.pone.0034318)

Based on the above study, what is the probability of elevated HMGB1 in colorectal cancer compared to the probability of elevated HMGB1 in a healthy control?

A. 20.1 %
B. 0.83
C. 5
D. 1.5

Explanation

This question is asking positive likelihood ratio (LR+) for the diagnostic test of HMGB1.
LR+ is the probability of a person who has the disease testing positive divided by the probability of a person who does not have the disease testing positive.
LR+ = sensitivity/ (1-specificity)
Sensitivity for HMGB1 = 20.1%
Specificity for HMGB1= 96%
= 20/(1-96) = 20/4 = 5 (The correct choice). The correct answer is C.

Negative likelihood ratio (LR-) is the probability of a person who has the disease testing negative divided by the probability of a person who does not have the disease testing negative.

LR- = (1-sensitivity)/specificity

In a 2x2 table, the calculation of likelihood ratio is shown below.

		Cervical Cancer by Gold standard test		Total	
		+ve	-ve		
Diagnostic Test	+ve	10 (True positive)	40 (False positive)	50	PPV= **True positive**/(True positive + False Positive)
	-ve	5 (False negative)	45 (True negative)	50	NPV= **True negative**/(True negative + False negative)
		15	85	100	
		Sensitivity= **True positive**/(True positive + False negative)	Specificity= **True negative**/(True negative + False Positive)		**LR+ = TPR/FPR**
					LR- = FNR/TNR

Take home message:

LR+ is the probability of a person who has the disease testing positive divided by the probability of a person who does not have the disease testing positive.

LR+ = sensitivity/ (1-specificity)

Question 24.

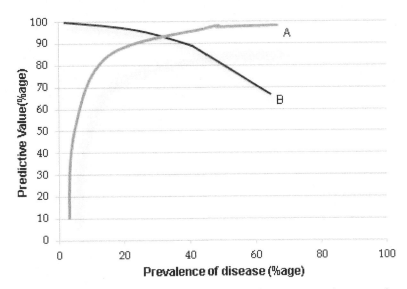

Prevalence of disease (%age)

What does the curve A in the figure above denote ?
A. Sensitivity
B. Specificity
C. Positive Predictive Value
D. Negative Predictive Value

The curve above shows the relationship of predictive values to that of prevalence of disease. As the prevalence of a disease increases, the positive predictive value (PPV) also increases. However, the negative predictive value decreases with prevalence (**curve B**). The correct answer is C.

$$PPV = \frac{sensitivity \times prevalence}{sensitivity \times prevalence + (1 - specificity) \times (1 - prevalence)}$$

$$NPV = \frac{specificity \times (1 - prevalence)}{(1 - sensitivity) \times prevalence + specificity \times (1 - prevalence)}$$

Take Home Message
As the prevalence of a disease increases, the positive predictive value also increases. However, the negative predictive value decreases with prevalence.

Question 25.

In a research study, a new diagnostic test that measures Substance X was evaluated for the diagnosis of cervical cancer. The data obtained was put in 2 x 2 table as follows:

		Cervical Cancer by Gold standard test		Total
		+ve	-ve	
Diagnostic Test	+ve	10	40	50
	-ve	5	45	50
		15	85	100

One of your patients who tested positive for substance X asks you what is the probability that she has cervical cancer. What would be your reply?

A. (10/15) x 100
B. (45/85) x 100
C. (10/50) x 100
D. (45/50) x 100

Explanation

This question is asking the positive predictive value of the new diagnostic test. Positive predictive value answers the question as to what proportion of all the positive test results are truly positive by gold standard tests.

		Cervical Cancer by Gold standard test		Total	
		+ve	-ve		
Diagnostic Test	+ve	10 (True positive)	40 (False positive)	50	PPV= **True positive**/(True positive + False Positive)
	-ve	5 (False negative)	45 (True negative)	50	NPV= **True negative**/(True negative + False negative)
		15	85	100	
		Sensitivity= **True positive**/(True positive + False negative)	Specificity= **True negative**/(True negative + False Positive)		

PPV= 10/ (10 + 40) x 100 (in %age) (Choice C). The correct answer is C.

Take Home Message

Positive predictive value answers the question as to what proportion of all the positive test results are truly positive by gold standard tests.

Question 26.

Research Abstract

Introduction

Neutrophil CD64 has been proposed as an early marker of sepsis. This study aims to evaluate the diagnostic utility of neutrophil CD64 for identification of early-onset sepsis in preterm neonates.

Methods

The prospective study was conducted in a neonatal intensive care unit between November 2010 and June 2011. Preterm neonates in whom infection was suspected when they were <12 hours of age were enrolled. Complete blood count with differential, blood culture, neutrophil CD11b and CD64 measurement were performed. Receiver operating characteristic curve analysis was performed to evaluate the performance of neutrophil CD64 as biomarker of sepsis.

Results

A total of 158 preterm neonates was enrolled, 88 of whom were suspected infection. The suspected sepsis group was of lesser gestational age ($P<0.001$) and lower birth weight ($P<0.001$), compared with controls. The hematologic profiles of the suspected sepsis group were characterized by higher white blood cell count, neutrophil counts and C-reactive protein. The suspected sepsis neonates had significantly higher neutrophil CD64 expression compared with controls. Neutrophil CD64 had an area value under the curve of 0.869 with an optimal cutoff values of 1010 phycoerythrin molecules bound/cell and it had a high sensitivity (82%) and negative predictive value (77.4%). The level of neutrophil CD64 was independent of antibiotic therapy within 24 hours after the onset of sepsis in preterm neonates.

Conclusions

Neutrophil CD64 is a highly sensitive marker for suspected early-onset sepsis in preterm neonates. Our study suggests that neutrophil CD64 may be incorporated as a valuable marker to diagnose infection.

Citation: Du J, Li L, Dou Y, Li P, Chen R, Liu H (2014) Diagnostic Utility of Neutrophil CD64 as a Marker for Early-Onset Sepsis in Preterm Neonates. PLoS ONE 9(7): e102647. doi:10.1371/journal.pone.0102647

Based on the study above, if 10 preterm neonates with suspected sepsis were tested for Neutrophil CD64 then what is the probability that at least one of the patients would test negative?

A. 1-0.82
B. 10 x 0.18
C. 1-(10 x 0.82)
D. 1- 0.82^{10}
E. 0.82

Explanation

This question is testing the concept of probability. Probability is the measure of the likeliness that an event will occur. Probability is quantified as a number between 0 and 1 (where 0 indicates impossibility and 1 indicates certainty).

The sensitivity (true positive rate) of Neutrophil CD64 for diagnosis of suspected sepsis is given in the research abstract as 82% or 0.82. This means that the probability that a septic neonate would test positive is 0.82. However, there is also a probability of (1-0.82= 0.18) that this septic neonates would test negative (i.e false negative rate is 18%). This probability is for 1 patient and not for all 10 of them.

In a question that asks "at least one" negative, only two possibilities exist.
A. Either all 10 are positive or
B. 9 are positive and "at least one" is negative

So,

P (all 10 are positive) = 0.82 x 0.82 x 0.82 x ....0.82 = 0.82^{10} (**multiplication rule for probability of independent events occurring together**)
P (9 are positive and "at least one" is negative) = X

P (either A or B) = 1= X + 0.82^{10} (**addition rule for probability of mutually exclusive events**)
Therefore,
P (9 are positive and "at least one" is negative) = X = 1- 0.82^{10} (**the correct answer**). The correct answer is D.

Take Home Message

Independent events

If two events, *A* and *B* are independent then the joint probability is

P (A and B) = P (A) x P(B)

Mutually exclusive events

If two events are mutually exclusive then the probability of either occurring is

P (A or B) = P (A) + P(B) = 1

Quantifying Risk

Question 27.

Research Abstract

Aims

To estimate the efficacy of standard and intensive statin treatment in the secondary prevention of major cardiovascular and cerebrovascular events in diabetes patients.

Methods

A systematic search was conducted in Medline over the years 1990 to September 2013. Randomized, double-blind, clinical trials comparing a standard-dose statin with placebo or a standard-dose statin with an intensive-dose statin for the secondary prevention of cardiovascular and cerebrovascular events in diabetes patients were selected. Trial and patient characteristics were extracted independently by two researchers. The combined effect on the composite primary endpoint was measured with a fixed-effect model. Potential publication bias was examined with a funnel plot.

Result

Figure. Results of the primary endpoint of major cardiovascular and cerebrovascular events comparing standard-dose statins with placebo.

Study or Subgroup	Experimental Events	Experimental Total	Control Events	Control Total	Weight
4S	46	105	61	97	7.0%
ASPEN	66	252	78	253	8.6%
CARE	81	282	112	304	11.9%
HPS	325	972	381	1009	41.2%
LIPID	245	542	282	535	31.3%
Total (95% CI)		2153		2198	100.0%
Total events	763		914		

Heterogeneity: Chi² = 3.14, df = 4 (P = 0.53); I² = 0%
Test for overall effect: Z = 4.33 (P < 0.0001)

Citation: de Vries FM, Kolthof J, Postma MJ, Denig P, Hak E (2014) Efficacy of Standard and Intensive Statin Treatment for the Secondary Prevention of Cardiovascular and Cerebrovascular Events in Diabetes Patients: A Meta-Analysis. PLoS ONE 9(11): e111247. doi:10.1371/journal.pone.0111247

How much risk of major cardiovascular and cerebrovascular events is attributable to standard dose statin when compared to placebo?

A. 85%

B. 70%

C. 6 %

D. 15%

Explanation:
The question is asking absolute risk reduction. **Absolute risk reduction (RRR)** is the difference in risk attributable to the intervention as compared to a control.
Let us put the values given in the figure in a 2x 2 table.

	Events		
	+	-	Total
Standard-dose statin	763	b	2153
Placebo	914	d	2198

Relative risk = risk of events in those on standard dose statin ÷ risk of events in those on placebo
Relative Risk = (a/a+b) ÷ (c/c+d)
$$= (763/2153) ÷ (914/2198)$$
$$= 0.85 \text{ or } 85 \% \textbf{ (Choice A)}$$
Absolute risk reduction = risk of events in those on placebo - risk of events in those on standard dose statin (**the difference in risk**)
= (914/2198) - (763/2153) = 0.06 or 6% (**The correct choice**)
Relative Risk Reduction = 1- RR = 1- 0.85 =0.15 = 15% (**Choice D**)

Take Home Message
Absolute risk reduction (RRR) is the difference in risk attributable to the intervention as compared to a control.

Question 28.

Research Abstract

Aims

To estimate the efficacy of standard and intensive statin treatment in the secondary prevention of major cardiovascular and cerebrovascular events in diabetes patients.

Methods

A systematic search was conducted in Medline over the years 1990 to September 2013. Randomized, double-blind, clinical trials comparing a standard-dose statin with placebo or a standard-dose statin with an intensive-dose statin for the secondary prevention of cardiovascular and cerebrovascular events in diabetes patients were selected. Trial and patient characteristics were extracted independently by two researchers. The combined effect on the composite primary endpoint was measured with a fixed-effect model. Potential publication bias was examined with a funnel plot.

Result

Figure. Results of the primary endpoint of major cardiovascular and cerebrovascular events comparing standard-dose statins with placebo.

Study or Subgroup	Experimental Events	Total	Control Events	Total	Weight
4S	46	105	61	97	7.0%
ASPEN	66	252	78	253	8.6%
CARE	81	282	112	304	11.9%
HPS	325	972	381	1009	41.2%
LIPID	245	542	282	535	31.3%
Total (95% CI)		2153		2198	100.0%
Total events	763		914		

Heterogeneity: $Chi^2 = 3.14$, $df = 4$ $(P = 0.53)$; $I^2 = 0\%$
Test for overall effect: $Z = 4.33$ $(P < 0.0001)$

Citation: de Vries FM, Kolthof J, Postma MJ, Denig P, Hak E (2014) Efficacy of Standard and Intensive Statin Treatment for the Secondary Prevention of Cardiovascular and Cerebrovascular Events in Diabetes Patients: A Meta-Analysis. PLoS ONE 9(11): e111247. doi:10.1371/journal.pone.0111247

Based on the data above, how many diabetes patients should be treated with standard-dose statin so that at least one patient benefits?

A. 27

B. 17

C. 6

D. 15

Explanation:
The question is asking "Number needed to treat".
Number needed to treat (**NNT**) is the number of patients who need to be treated in order for 1 patient to benefit.
NNT = 1/ARR where ARR is absolute risk reduction

ARR= Absolute risk reduction = risk of events in those on placebo - risk of events in those on standard dose statin (**the difference in risk**)
= (914/2198) - (763/2153) = 0.06 or 6%

Therefore,
NNT = 1/0.06 = 17 (**The correct answer**).

Contrast this with **number needed to harm (NNH).**

NNH = 1/AR where AR is attributable risk.

Attributable risk is the difference in risk between exposed and unexposed.

NNH and AR deals with **risk factors rather than intervention**.

Take Home Message

Number needed to treat (**NNT**) is the number of patients who need to be treated in order for 1 patient to benefit.

NNT = 1/ARR where ARR is absolute risk reduction

Question 29.

In their article published in J Can Acad Child Adolesc Psychiatry. 2008 Nov; 17(4): 197–201, Greenfield and colleagues looked at previously suicidal adolescents (n=263) and analyzed the data to determine the associations between baseline variables such as age, sex, presence of psychiatric disorder, previous hospitalizations, and drug and alcohol use, with suicidal behavior at six-month follow-up. Suicidal ideation and/or attempts were measured using the Pfeffer's Spectrum of Suicidal Behavior Scale (PSSBS) (Pfeffer, 1986), which measures suicidal behavior on a five-point scale (1: nonsuicidal, 2: suicidal ideation, 3: suicidal threat, 4: mild attempt, 5: serious attempt).The non-suicidal group (NS) at follow-up (PSSBS=1, n=186, 71%) was compared to the suicidal group (S) (PSSBS>1, n=77, 29%) with respect to baseline measures. The data that they got is shown in the table below.

Table 1

Clinical characteristics of the suicidal adolescents at baseline and between-group differences

Characteristic	Suicidal (S) (n=77) % or mean±SD	Non-Suicidal (NS) (n=186) % or mean±SD
Age	14.7 ± 1.4	14.5 ± 1.6
Sex (female)	79.2	64.0
IFR score	46.1 ± 23.8	42.4 ± 24.7
Depression	58.4	46.2
Conduct disorder	32.5	19.8
Life events	11.7 ± 7.0	10.2 ± 6.6
Number of previous hospitalization	0.5 ± 0.7	0.3 ± 0.5
Borderline personality disorder	90.9	72.6
Previous suicide attempt(s)	89.6	71.6
Drug use	71.4	45.9
Alcohol use	63.3	48.8
CGAS score	38.6 ± 11.5	40.0 ± 11.0
Parent previous suicide attempt(s)	87.5	78.7
Parental psychopathology	40.3	38.7
Living arrangement (group home)	5.4	4.0
Compliance to treatment	28.6	37.6

What is the odds that the group who were suicidal at 6 months follow-up had depression at baseline?

A. 1.0
B. 2.0
C. 3.8
D. 3.0
E. 1.6

Explanation

Odds ratio is used in case-control study. To calculate odds ratio, we first need to create a 2 x 2 frequency table.

		Outcome Status	
		+	-
Exposure	+	a	b

Status	-	c	d
		a+c	b+d

a = those who were exposed to baseline variables (in this case, had depression) and were determined suicidal (+) at 6 month follow-up = 58.4 % of 77 (see Table) = 45

b = those who were exposed to baseline variables (in this case, had depression) and were determined to be non-suicidal (-) at 6 month follow-up = 46.2% of 186 (see Table) = 86

c = those who were not exposed (-) to baseline variables (in this case, did not have depression) and were determined suicidal (+) at 6 month follow-up = (a+c)-a = 77- 45 = 32

d = those who were not exposed (-) to baseline variables (in this case, did not have depression) and were determined non-suicidal(-) at 6 month follow-up = (b+d)- b =186-86= 100

Putting these values in the table gives us:

		Outcome Status	
		Suicidal	Non-suicidal
Exposure Status	Depression	45	86
	No depression	32	100
		77	186

Odds ratio = Odds that suicidal group had depression at baseline/ odds that non-suicidal group had depression

= a/c ÷ b/d = 45/32 ÷ 86/100 = 1.40 ÷0.86 = **1.63 (The correct answer)**

Another approach to answer this question is to use percentages.

Putting these percentages in the table gives us:

		Outcome Status	
		Suicidal	Non-suicidal
Exposure Status	Depression	58.4	46.2
	No depression	41.6	53.8
		100	100

Odds ratio = Odds that suicidal group had depression at baseline/ odds that non-suicidal group had depression

= a/c ÷ b/d = 58.4/41.6 ÷ 46.2/53.8 = 1.40 ÷0.86 = **1.63 (The correct answer)**

Question 30.

Research Abstract

Aims

To estimate the efficacy of standard and intensive statin treatment in the secondary prevention of major cardiovascular and cerebrovascular events in diabetes patients.

Methods

A systematic search was conducted in Medline over the years 1990 to September 2013. Randomized, double-blind, clinical trials comparing a standard-dose statin with placebo or a standard-dose statin with an intensive-dose statin for the secondary prevention of cardiovascular and cerebrovascular events in diabetes patients were selected. Trial and patient characteristics were extracted independently by two researchers. The combined effect on the composite primary endpoint was measured with a fixed-effect model. Potential publication bias was examined with a funnel plot.

Result

Figure. Results of the primary endpoint of major cardiovascular and cerebrovascular events comparing standard-dose statins with placebo.

Study or Subgroup	Experimental Events	Total	Control Events	Total	Weight
4S	46	105	61	97	7.0%
ASPEN	66	252	78	253	8.6%
CARE	81	282	112	304	11.9%
HPS	325	972	381	1009	41.2%
LIPID	245	542	282	535	31.3%
Total (95% CI)		2153		2198	100.0%
Total events	763		914		

Heterogeneity: Chi² = 3.14, df = 4 (P = 0.53); I² = 0%
Test for overall effect: Z = 4.33 (P < 0.0001)

Citation: de Vries FM, Kolthof J, Postma MJ, Denig P, Hak E (2014) Efficacy of Standard and Intensive Statin Treatment for the Secondary Prevention of Cardiovascular and Cerebrovascular Events in Diabetes Patients: A Meta-Analysis. PLoS ONE 9(11): e111247. doi:10.1371/journal.pone.0111247

When compared to placebo, by what percentage does standard-dose statin decreases the risk of major cardiovascular and cerebrovascular events?

A. 85%

B. 70%

C. 30 %

D. 15%

Explanation:

The question is asking relative risk reduction. **Relative risk reduction (RRR)** is the proportion of risk reduction attributable to the intervention as compared to a control. Let us put the values given in the figure in a 2x 2 table.

	Events		
	+	-	Total
Standard-dose statin	763	b	2153
Placebo	914	d	2198

Relative risk = risk of events in those on standard dose statin ÷ risk of events in those on placebo

Relative Risk = (a/a+b) ÷ (c/c+d)

$$= (763/2153) ÷ (914/2198)$$
$$= 0.85$$

Relative Risk Reduction = 1- RR = 1- 0.85 =0.15 = 15% (**Choice D**)

Take Home Message
Relative risk reduction (RRR) is the proportion of risk reduction attributable to the intervention as compared to control.

Statistical Distribution

Question 31.

In a patient with diabetic ketoacidosis in ICU, K level is measured every hour. His K+ levels are as follows:

6.0
5.7
5.7
5.6
5.6
5.5
5.5
5.5
5.4
5.3
7.0

Which of the following is not affected by the last value of 7.0 meq/L?

A. Mean
B. Median
C. Mode
D. Sample Standard Deviation
E. Variance

Explanation

Outliers are observations that are abnormally high or low in a set of observations. In the above example, 7.0 is abnormally higher than all the other values and hence is an outlier.

Mean, Median and Mode are the three primary measures of central tendency. Standard Deviations and Variations are derived from mean.
Mean
Mean is the arithmetic mean of a data set obtained by summing up all the values in the data set and dividing them by the number of observations.

In the example, the mean with and without the outlier would be as follows.

Mean = (6.0 + 5.7 + 5.7 + 5.6 + 5.6 + 5.5 + 5.5 + 5.5 + 5.4 + 5.3 + 7.0)/2 = **31.4**
Mean(without the outlier 7.0) = (6.0 + 5.7 + 5.7 + 5.6 + 5.6 + 5.5 + 5.5 + 5.5 + 5.4 + 5.3)/2 = **27.9**
Median
Median is the middle value of a data set sorted in ascending or descending order. If the number of observations are even number, then median is the average of the middle two values.
In the example, we have odd number of observations of 11. The middle value will be at (n+1)/2 = (11+1)/2 = 6
Sorting the values in ascending order gives us:
5.3, 5.4, 5.5., 5.5, 5.5, **5.6**, 5.6, 5.7, 5.7, 6.0, 7.0
Median = 5.6

In the example if we remove the outlier 7.0, we have even number of observations of 10. The middle value will be at (n+1)/2 = (10+1)/2 = 5.5
Sorting the values in ascending order gives us:
5.3, 5.4, 5.5., 5.5, **5.5**, **5.6**, 5.6, 5.7, 5.7, 6.0

The middle two values in this even number of observations are 5.5 and 5.6 . Median would be the average of the two.
Median= (5.5 + 5.6)/2 = 5.55
Mode

Mode is the most frequently occurring value in a data set. A frequency table helps in determining the Mode.

In this small data set, eyeballing shows that 5.5 is repeated three times, more then any other value, and hence is the Mode. The outlier of 7.0 does not affect this value.

As a rule, median is always resistant to outliers. The mode is generally resistant unless there are several mode such as bimodal, trimodal and so on and happens to include outliers.

Question 32.

Abstract

Lipid levels in patients hospitalized with coronary artery disease: an analysis of 136,905 hospitalizations in Get With The Guidelines.

Sachdeva A1, Cannon CP, Deedwania PC, Labresh KA, Smith SC Jr, Dai D, Hernandez A, Fonarow GC.

Am Heart J. 2009 Jan;157(1):111-117.e2.

BACKGROUND:

Lipid levels among contemporary patients hospitalized with coronary artery disease (CAD) have not been well studied. This study aimed to analyze admission lipid levels in a broad contemporary population of patients hospitalized with CAD.

METHODS:

The Get With The Guidelines database was analyzed for CAD hospitalizations from 2000 to 2006 with documented lipid levels in the first 24 hours of admission. Patients were divided into low-density lipoprotein cholesterol (LDL), high-density lipoprotein cholesterol (HDL), and triglyceride categories. Factors associated with LDL and HDL levels were assessed along with temporal trends.

RESULTS:

Of 231,986 hospitalizations from 541 hospitals, admission lipid levels were documented in 136,905 (59.0%). Mean lipid levels were LDL 104.9 +/- 39.8, HDL 39.7 +/- 13.2, and triglyceride 161 +/- 128 mg/dL(mean +/- SD). Low-density lipoprotein cholesterol <70 mg/dL was observed in 17.6% and ideal levels (LDL <70 with HDL > or =60 mg/dL) in only 1.4%. High-density lipoprotein cholesterol was <40 mg/dL in 54.6% of patients. Before admission, only 28,944 (21.1%) patients were receiving lipid-lowering medications. Predictors for higher LDL included female gender, no diabetes, history of hyperlipidemia, no prior lipid-lowering medications, and presenting with acute coronary syndrome. Both LDL and HDL levels declined over time (P < .0001).

CONCLUSIONS:

In a large cohort of patients hospitalized with CAD, almost half have admission LDL levels <100 mg/dL. More than half the patients have admission HDL levels <40 mg/dL, whereas <10% have HDL > or =60 mg/dL. These findings may provide further support for recent guideline revisions with even lower LDL goals and for developing effective treatments to raise HDL.

The distributions of admission LDL is shown in Figure below.

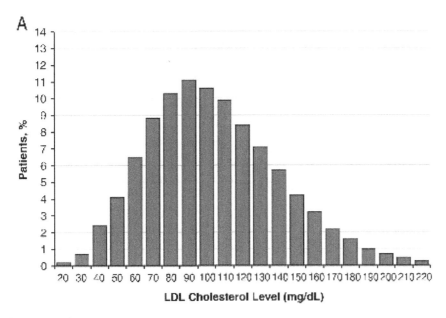

Figure 1

Distribution of admission LDL, HDL, and triglyceride levels. (**A**) Histogram of admission LDL levels in 10 mg/dL increments.

In this study, 95% of the patients had admission LDL level between approximately which of the following?

A. 25.3 and 184.5 mg/dl
B. 50 and 200 mg/dl
C. 65.1 and 144.7 mg/dl
D. -14.5 and 224.3 mg/dl
E. 70 and 200 mg/dl

Explanation:

The result section of this abstract says that the admission LDL level was 104.9 +/- 39.8 (mean +/- SD)
The histogram looks more or less bell-shaped. Bell-shaped histogram are said to be normally distributed.

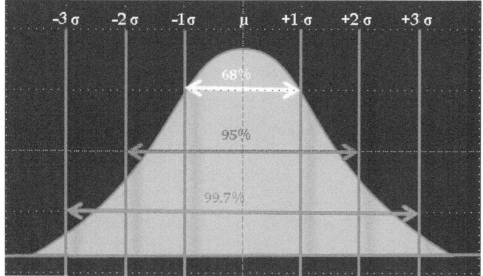

As we can see in the above figure, the percentage of data that are within 2 standard deviation (+/- 2 σ) is 95 %.
Therefore, 95% of the patients will have admission LDL values between mean +/- 2 σ .
Mean is 104.9 and 1 σ (or SD) is 39.8.
Hence, the correct answer would be 104.9 +/- (2 x 39.8) (i.e 65.1 and 144.7 mg/dl).

Other important points to remember:
In a normal distribution,
Means= mode = median
Mode is always the highest point in a distribution curve as it is the value that occurs most often in a set of data.
Mode and Median are resistant to outliers. Median is always resistant. Mode is not resistant when several outliers become Mode.
Median is the middle value in a given sequence of data (ascending or descending). In case there is an even number of values, the median is the average of the middle two values.
Take Home Message

In a normal distribution, the percentage of data that are within 2 standard deviation (+/- 2 σ) is 95 %.

Question 33.

Abstract

Lipid levels in patients hospitalized with coronary artery disease: an analysis of 136,905 hospitalizations in Get With The Guidelines.

Sachdeva A1, Cannon CP, Deedwania PC, Labresh KA, Smith SC Jr, Dai D, Hernandez A, Fonarow GC.

Am Heart J. 2009 Jan;157(1):111-117.e2.

BACKGROUND:

Lipid levels among contemporary patients hospitalized with coronary artery disease (CAD) have not been well studied. This study aimed to analyze admission lipid levels in a broad contemporary population of patients hospitalized with CAD.

METHODS:

The Get With The Guidelines database was analyzed for CAD hospitalizations from 2000 to 2006 with documented lipid levels in the first 24 hours of admission. Patients were divided into low-density lipoprotein cholesterol (LDL), high-density lipoprotein cholesterol (HDL), and triglyceride categories. Factors associated with LDL and HDL levels were assessed along with temporal trends.

RESULTS:

Of 231,986 hospitalizations from 541 hospitals, admission lipid levels were documented in 136,905 (59.0%). Mean lipid levels were LDL 104.9 +/- 39.8, HDL 39.7 +/- 13.2, and triglyceride 161 +/- 128 mg/dL(mean +/- SD). Low-density lipoprotein cholesterol <70 mg/dL was observed in 17.6% and ideal levels (LDL <70 with HDL > or =60 mg/dL) in only 1.4%. High-density lipoprotein cholesterol was <40 mg/dL in 54.6% of patients. Before admission, only 28,944 (21.1%) patients were receiving lipid-lowering medications. Predictors for higher LDL included female gender, no diabetes, history of hyperlipidemia, no prior lipid-lowering medications, and presenting with acute coronary syndrome. Both LDL and HDL levels declined over time (P < .0001).

CONCLUSIONS:

In a large cohort of patients hospitalized with CAD, almost half have admission LDL levels <100 mg/dL. More than half the patients have admission HDL levels <40 mg/dL, whereas <10% have HDL > or =60 mg/dL. These findings may provide further support for recent guideline revisions with even lower LDL goals and for developing effective treatments to raise HDL.

The distribution of HDL and Triglyceride levels is shown in the figure below.

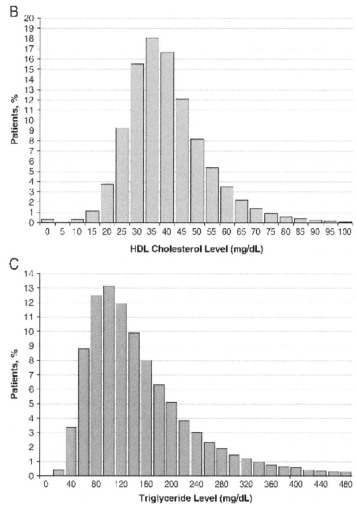

Figure 1

Distribution of admission HDL and triglyceride levels. (**B**) Histogram of admission HDL levels in 5 mg/dL increments. (**C**) Histogram of admission triglyceride levels in 20 mg/dL increments (truncated at 480 mg/dL).

What is the mode for triglyceride level in the above study based on the figure above?
A. 161 mg/dl
B. 100 mg/dl
C. 250 mg/dl
D. 130 mg/dl

E. 40 mg/dl

Explanation

Mode is the most frequently occurring value in a set of observation.

A distribution can be nonnormal such as Bimodal, Positive Skew or Negative Skew.

Bimodal

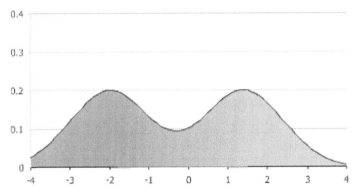

Image Credit: https://en.wikipedia.org/wiki/Multimodal_distribution

Examples:

1. The rate of suicide was highest among adults between 45 and 54 years of age and then second peak was seen in those 85 years or older.

2. Bimodal distribution of isoniazid half-lives caused by rapid and slow acetylation of the drug.

3. Incidence of Hodgkins Lymphoma has bimodal distribution as it has two peaks, one at the 3rd and the second at the 6th decade of life.

Skewed distributions

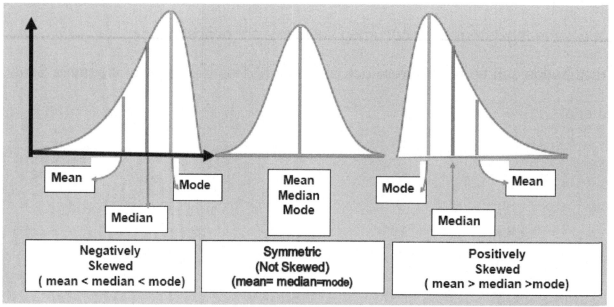

Statistical Hypothesis

Question 34.

Endothelin receptor-A antagonist attenuates retinal vascular and neuroretinal pathology in diabetic mice.

Chou JC, Rollins SD, Ye M, Batlle D, Fawzi AA.

Invest Ophthalmol Vis Sci. 2014 Apr 17;55(4):2516-25.

Abstract

PURPOSE:

We sought to determine the effects of atrasentan, a selective endothelin-A receptor antagonist, on the retinal vascular and structural integrity in a db/db mouse, an animal model of type 2 diabetes and diabetic retinopathy.

METHODS:

Diabetic mice, 23 weeks old, were given either atrasentan or vehicle treatment in drinking water for 8 weeks. At the end of the treatment period, eyes underwent trypsin digest to assess the retinal vascular pathology focusing on capillary degeneration, endothelial cell, and pericyte loss. Paraffin-embedded retinal cross sections were used to evaluate retinal sublayer thickness both near the optic nerve and in the retinal periphery. Immunohistochemistry and TUNEL assay were done to evaluate retinal cellular and vascular apoptosis.

RESULTS:

Compared with untreated db/db mice, atrasentan treatment was able to ameliorate the retinal vascular pathology by reducing pericyte loss (29.2% ± 0.4% vs. 44.4% ± 2.0%, respectively, $P < 0.05$) and capillary degeneration as determined by the percentage of acellular capillaries (8.6% ± 0.3% vs. 3.3% ± 0.41%, respectively, $P < 0.05$). A reduction in inner retinal thinning both at the optic nerve and at the periphery in treated diabetic mice was also observed in db/db mice treated with atrasentan as compared with untreated db/db mice ($P < 0.05$). TUNEL assay suggested that atrasentan may decrease enhanced apoptosis in neuroretinal layers and vascular pericytes in the db/db mice.

CONCLUSIONS:

Endothelin-A receptor blockade using atrasentan significantly reduces the vascular and neuroretinal complications in diabetic mice. Endothelin-A receptor blockade is a promising therapeutic target in diabetic retinopathy.

Table 1

Summary of Metabolic Status and Vascular Changes

Group	Body Weight, g	Blood Glucose, mg/dL	E/P Ratio	Endothelial Cell Density*	Pericyte Density*	Acellular Capillary†
db/m, $n = 8$	$27 \pm 0.7\ddagger$	$164 \pm 12\ddagger$	$3.73 \pm 0.28\S$	50.0 ± 1.3	$50.0 \pm 1.3\S$	$2.7 \pm 0.3\S$
db/db, $n = 9$	57.7 ± 2.0	398 ± 64	6.63 ± 0.41	55.4 ± 2.2	29.2 ± 0.4	8.6 ± 0.3
db/db, atrasentan, $n = 8$	56.1 ± 1.9	272 ± 52	$4.35 \pm 0.19\|\|$	52.9 ± 1.8	$44.4 \pm 2.0\|\|$	$3.3 \pm 0.4\|\|$

* Capillary density: Values are normalized to control db/m mice and are based on the number of reticle squares needed to count 50 endothelial cells (87) and pericytes (207) in db/m.

† Acellular capillaries (per five retinal fields).

‡ Reflects a statistically significant difference ($P < 0.05$) comparing db/m to untreated db/db group. There was no statistically significant difference in blood glucose between db/m and atrasentan-treated db/db mice (see text). No significant differences were found between the two db/db groups regarding body weight or blood glucose.

§ Reflects that db/m mice are significantly different from db/db mice.

|| Reflects that atrasentan-treated db/db mice are significantly different from the untreated db/db group, but not different from db/m mice.

In the above study, T-test showed a Type 1 error of > 5% in terms of detecting difference in glucose level between db/db mouse treated with vehicle and those treated with Atrasentan. What can be done to reduce type 2 error?

A. Decrease effect size
B. Increase sample size
C. Decrease power of study
D. Decrease sample size

Explanation

Null Hypothesis states that there is no statistical difference between the group. Alternate Hypothesis states that there is a statistical difference.

		Alternate Hypothesis(H_1) is true in reality	Null Hypothesis (H_0) is true in reality
		H_1	H_0
	H_1 (Conclusion you draw from the data is reject the null hypothesis)	Good conclusion $(1-\beta)$	Type 1 Error (α)
STUDY RESULTS	H_0 (Conclusion you draw from the data is to accept the null hypothesis)	Type 2 Error (β)	Good Conclusion

Statistical Hypothesis tests determine the probability of making Type 1 error (aka α error or p value). If its < 5% (or <0.05), then the difference between study groups is considered significant.

In the above study,
Mean glucose in vehicle-treated db/db mice is 398
Mean glucose in Atrasentan-treated db/db mice is 272
So the study result shows a difference of 398-272 = 126

If we do not do statistical hypotheses tests, we will draw the conclusion that there is a difference in glucose level between the two groups. In other words, you will reject null hypothesis (H0) and accept alternate hypothesis (H1).

Statistical tests in the above study shows that Type 1 error is > 5% (i.e p value >0.05). This means that the probability that we could have observed this difference of 126 if the null hypothesis were true is >5 %. Hence, the difference is not significant.

In any study, we want the power of study to be >= 80%. Power of a study is the ability of a study to detect a significant difference or in other words to correctly reject null hypotheses when alternate hypotheses is true in reality. In the above study, to make sure that the difference of 126 that we are seeing is true in reality (and not by chance), we have to increase the power of the study.

Power of the study $(1-\beta)$ depends on sample size and effect size. Type 2 error (β) can be reduced by increasing sample size (Choice B).

Take Home Message
Power of the study $(1-\beta)$ depends on sample size and effect size.

Outcomes of statistical hypothesis testing

Question 35.

In their article published in J Can Acad Child Adolesc Psychiatry. 2008 Nov; 17(4): 197–201, Greenfield and colleagues looked at previously suicidal adolescents (n=263) and analyzed the data to determine the associations between baseline variables such as age, sex, presence of psychiatric disorder, previous hospitalizations, and drug and alcohol use, with suicidal behavior at six-month follow-up. Suicidal ideation and/or attempts were measured using the Pfeffer's Spectrum of Suicidal Behavior Scale (PSSBS) (Pfeffer, 1986), which measures suicidal behavior on a five-point scale (1: nonsuicidal, 2: suicidal ideation, 3: suicidal threat, 4: mild attempt, 5: serious attempt).The non-suicidal group (NS) at follow-up (PSSBS=1, n=186, 71%) was compared to the suicidal group (S) (PSSBS>1, n=77, 29%) with respect to baseline measures. The data that they got is shown in the table below.

Table 1

Clinical characteristics of the suicidal adolescents at baseline and between-group differences

Characteristic	Suicidal (S) (n=77) % or mean±SD	Non-Suicidal (NS) (n=186) % or mean±SD	Odds Ratio) (S/NS)	95% C.I.
Age	14.7 ± 1.4	14.5 ± 1.6	1.1	0.9 – 1.3
Sex (female)	79.2	64.0	2.2	1.2 – 4.0
IFR score	46.1 ± 23.8	42.4 ± 24.7	1.0	1.0 – 1.0
Depression	58.4	46.2	1.6	1.0 – 2.8
Conduct disorder	32.5	19.8	2.0	1.1 – 3.6
Life events	11.7 ± 7.0	10.2 ± 6.6	1.0	1.0 – 1.1
Number of previous hospitalization	0.5 ± 0.7	0.3 ± 0.5	1.6	1.1 – 2.5
Borderline personality disorder	90.9	72.6	3.8	1.6 – 8.7
Previous suicide attempt(s)	89.6	71.6	3.4	1.2 – 9.6
Drug use	71.4	45.9	3.0	1.7 – 5.2
Alcohol use	63.3	48.8	1.8	0.9 – 3.6
CGAS score	38.6 ± 11.5	40.0 ± 11.0	1.0	1.0 – 1.0
Parent previous suicide attempt(s)	87.5	78.7	1.9	0.5 – 7.7
Parental psychopathology	40.3	38.7	1.1	0.6 – 1.8
Living arrangement (group home)	5.4	4.0	1.4	0.4 – 4.8
Compliance to treatment	28.6	37.6	0.7	0.8 – 1.2

Based on the study above, patients with which of the following baseline parameters have the significant odds of becoming suicidal in the next 6 months?

A. Age
B. Previous suicide attempt(s)
C. Alcohol
D. Depression
E. Parent Previous suicide attempt(s)

Explanation

Of the choices given, only "Previous suicide attempt(s)" has the 95% confidence interval (CI) for the odds ratio that does not include 1. The correct answer is B.
Rule of thumb is if the 95% CI for odds ratio or relative risk includes 1 then null hypothesis is not rejected. In other words, the ratio is not significantly different.

The other baseline parameters wherein CI does not include 1 are as follows:
Sex, Conduct disorder, number of previous hospitalizations, borderline personality disorder, previous suicide attempt(s), drug use
95 % CI is used to denote significance. However, the best way to determine significance is to calculate p values (see Table below).
95% Confidence Interval is the range of values in which a 95% of the odds of repeated samples would be expected to fall.

Calculation of Confidence Interval for means is as follows:
CI= mean – Z (SEM)   to   mean+ Z(SEM)
Z for 95% CI = 1.96
SEM is standard error of mean
SEM= SD/ square root (N) where SD is standard deviation and N is sample size.

Table 1

Clinical characteristics of the suicidal adolescents at baseline and between-group differences

Characteristic	Suicidal (S) (n=77) % or mean±SD	Non-Suicidal (NS) (n=186) % or mean±SD	Odds Ratio) (S/NS)	p-value	95% C.I.
Age	14.7 ± 1.4	14.5 ± 1.6	1.1	0.34	0.9 – 1.3
Sex (female)	79.2	64.0	2.2	0.02	1.2 – 4.0
IFR score	46.1 ± 23.8	42.4 ± 24.7	1.0	0.27	1.0 – 1.0
Depression	58.4	46.2	1.6	0.07	1.0 – 2.8
Conduct disorder	32.5	19.8	2.0	0.03	1.1 – 3.6
Life events	11.7 ± 7.0	10.2 ± 6.6	1.0	0.10	1.0 – 1.1
Number of previous hospitalization	0.5 ± 0.7	0.3 ± 0.5	1.6	0.03	1.1 – 2.5
Borderline personality disorder	90.9	72.6	3.8	0.002	1.6 – 8.7
Previous suicide attempt(s)	89.6	71.6	3.4	0.02	1.2 – 9.6
Drug use	71.4	45.9	3.0	0.001	1.7 – 5.2
Alcohol use	63.3	48.8	1.8	0.09	0.9 – 3.6
CGAS score	38.6 ± 11.5	40.0 ± 11.0	1.0	0.37	1.0 – 1.0
Parent previous suicide attempt(s)	87.5	78.7	1.9	0.37	0.5 – 7.7
Parental psychopathology	40.3	38.7	1.1	0.82	0.6 – 1.8
Living arrangement (group home)	5.4	4.0	1.4	0.63	0.4 – 4.8
Compliance to treatment	28.6	37.6	0.7	0.16	0.8 – 1.2

Take Home Message

Rule of thumb is if the 95% CI for odds ratio or relative risk includes 1 then null hypothesis is not rejected. In other words, the ratio is not significantly different.

Tests of Statistical Significance

Question 36.

fMRI study of the role of glutamate NMDA receptor in the olfactory processing in monkeys

Cardiorespiratory parameters during the 4-h experimental period (mean ± SD, n = 4).

(**A & B**) MK801 has no significant effect on the heart rate and blood oxygen saturation (SpO2). (**C**) MK801 significantly increased the respiration rate. The asterisks (*) indicate statistical differences comparing the respiration rate before MK801 injection.

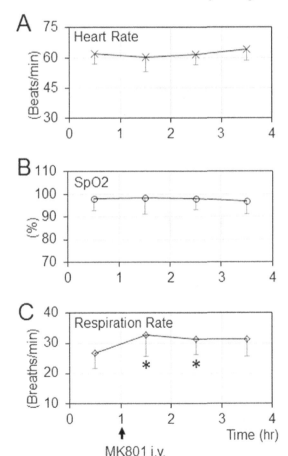

What statistical test should be used to determine statistical significance following MK801 i.v. injection?

    A. Chi Square Test

B. Unpaired T Test

C. Paired T Test

D. ANOVA

Explanations:

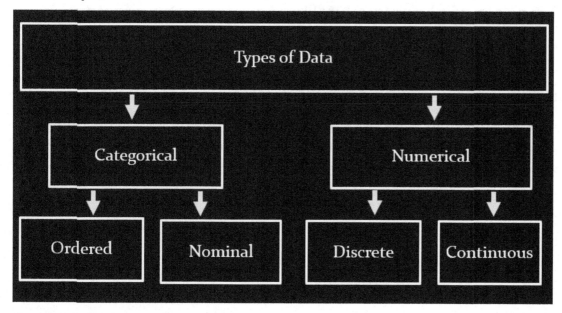

Comparing Categorical Data

Categorical variables represent types of data which may be divided into groups. Examples of categorical variables are race, sex, age group, and educational level.

Chi- Square: It is used to determine whether there is a significant difference between two proportions

Comparing Continuous Data

Continuous data can be measures and includes decimals such as LDL level in serum.

t-Test: It is used to determine whether there is a significant difference between the means of two groups. There are two types of t-Test. They are Paired and Unpaired t-Test. Example:

Paired T-Test : Comparing means of blood pressure in a group before and after an intervention. Choice C is the answer because we are comparing means before and after MK801 injection.

Unpaired t-Test: Comparing means of blood pressure in two independent group such as male vs female

Analysis of Variance (ANOVA): It is used to determine whether there is a significant difference between the means of three or more groups.

Useful Resources for USMLE Examinations

USMLE Step 1

First Aid for the USMLE Step 1 2018, 28th Edition
USMLE Step 1 Lecture Notes 2018: 7-Book Set (Kaplan Test Prep)
Biostatistics MCQs and Explanations for USMLE: 2019 Edition

USMLE Step 2 CK

Master the Boards USMLE Step 2 CK
Master the Boards USMLE Step 3
Biostatistics MCQs and Explanations for USMLE: 2019 Edition

USMLE Step 2 CS

First Aid for the USMLE Step 2 CS, Sixth Edition

USMLE Step 3

Master the Boards USMLE Step 3
Biostatistics MCQs and Explanations for USMLE: 2019 Edition

Made in the USA
Middletown, DE
13 October 2021